FOOTBALL
FACT BOOK

CARLING

FOOTBALL FACT BOOK

Henry Russell

Cartoons by
Peter Coupe

STOPWATCH

Published by Stopwatch Publishing Limited
For Bookmart Limited
Registered Number 2372865
Trading as Bookmart Limited
Desford Road
Enderby
Leicester
LE9 5AD

This edition published 1998

The views and opinions of the writer in this book are not necessarily those of Bass Brewers Limited

Printed and bound in Great Britain

Compiled by Henry Russell

© Stopwatch Publishing Limited
1-7 Shand Street
London SE1 2ES

info@stopwatch.co.uk

ISBN 1 900032 87 2

CONTENTS

THE DAWN OF TIME

The first England versus Scotland match was played at The Oval, Kennington, London on March 5, 1870. The two teams drew 1-1.

The first FA Cup was won by The Wanderers, who beat The Royal Engineers 1-0 in the Final at the Kennington Oval on March 16, 1872.

The winning goal in the first FA Cup Final was scored by M.P. Betts.

The Cup-winning Wanderers captain, C.W. Alcock, was also Secretary of the Football Association.

The first FA Cup had 15 entrants.

The FA Cup itself was known throughout the game as The Little Tin Idol. It was 18 inches high, had two curved handles and was crowned with a figure of a footballer on the lid.

The Cup had been made by Martin, Hall & Co and cost £20.

Queen's Park of Glasgow - Scotland's first football club - took part in the first English FA Cup, and received byes to the semi-final.

In the semi-final, Queen's Park drew with The Wanderers but could not afford to stay in London for the replay, so had to scratch from the tournament.

The first Scotland versus England match was played at the West of Scotland Cricket Ground, Partick on November 30, 1872. The final score was 0-0.

The first official international between England and Scotland was played at The Oval, Kennington, London on March 8, 1873. The score was England 4 Scotland 2.

The scorer of England's first ever international goal was Alexander Bonsor of Old Etonians and The Wanderers.

In March 1873, the Scots founded a Football Association and inaugurated their own FA Cup.

The first Scottish FA Cup trophy and badges cost £56.12s. 11d (about £56.64p).

In 1876, the Welsh FA was formed and Wales played their first international football match - they lost 4-0 to Scotland in Glasgow.

The first recorded match under electric lights was played on October 14, 1878, at Bramall Lane, Sheffield, between sides captained by the brothers J.C. and W.E. Clegg, both England internationals. 20,000 people are thought to have been present.

The first official football match in Northern Ireland was an exhibition game between the Scottish clubs Queen's Park and Caledonians on October 24, 1878.

1878 was also the year in which referees used whistles for the first time.

FA Cup Finals of the 1870s

1872	The Wanderers	1	Royal Engineers	0
1873	The Wanderers	2	Oxford University	0
1874	Oxford University	2	Royal Engineers	0
1875	Royal Engineers	1	Old Etonians	1
	Replay			
	Royal Engineers	2	Old Etonians	0
1876	The Wanderers	1	Old Etonians	1
	Replay			
	The Wanderers	3	Old Etonians	0
1877	The Wanderers	2	Oxford University	1(aet)
1878	The Wanderers	3	Royal Engineers	1
1879	Old Etonians	1	Clapham Rovers	0

Scottish FA Cup Finals of the 1870s

1874	Queen's Park	2	Clydesdale	0
1875	Queen's Park	3	Renton	0
1876	Queen's Park	1	Third Lanark	1
	Replay			
	Queen's Park	2	Third Lanark	0
1877	Vale of Leven	0	Rangers	0
	Replays			
	Vale of Leven	1	Rangers	1
	Vale of Leven	3	Rangers	2
1878	Vale of Leven	1	Third Lanark	0
1879	Vale of Leven	1	Rangers	1

(Vale of Leven then won the Cup by default when Rangers refused to take part in a replay because they had had a goal disallowed in the first match.)

In 1879, at the age of 17 years 245 days, James Prinsep of Clapham Rovers became the youngest man ever to appear in an FA Cup Final.

In 1883, the FA Cup went north for the first time, when Blackburn Olympic beat the Old Etonians 2-1 after extra time.

Blackburn Olympic retained the Cup the following year, 1884, but in 1885 the trophy was won by their neighbours, Blackburn Rovers, who beat Queen's Park 2-1 in the Final.

Blackburn Rovers then won the FA Cup three years running - they beat Queen's Park again 2-0 in the 1885 Final, then West Bromwich Albion 2-0 in a replay at the Racecourse Ground, Derby, after the first match at the Oval had been drawn 0-0.

The first Home International Championship was contested in 1884. Scotland won it with a clean sweep, beating Wales 4-1 in Glasgow, Ireland 5-0 in Belfast and England 1-0 at Cathkin Park, Glasgow.

The record score in any British first-class football match was Arbroath's 36-0 victory over Bon Accord in the Scottish FA Cup on September 5, 1885.

Arbroath winger John Petrie scored 13 goals in this match - a scoring record that still stands.

England's first professional footballer was James Forrest, who was paid to play against Scotland in 1885.

Scotland dominated the Home International Championship until 1886, when they shared the title with England.

In the first all-Midlands FA Cup Final in 1887, Aston Villa beat West Bromwich Albion 2-0 at Kennington Oval.

On their way to the trophy, Aston Villa had beaten Glasgow Rangers 3-1 in the semi-final.

In 1888, the winners of the English and Scottish FA Cups played each other for what was billed as 'The Championship of the World'. Renton beat West Bromwich Albion 2-1.

England won the Home International Championship outright for the first time in 1888, beating Ireland 5-1, Wales 5-1 and Scotland 5-0.

On April 17, 1888, the Football League was founded after a meeting at the Royal Hotel, Manchester. The mastermind - often known as The Father of League Football - was William McGregor, a director of Aston Villa.

The twelve founder members of the English Football League were Accrington, Aston Villa, Blackburn Rovers, Bolton Wanderers, Burnley, Derby County, Everton, Notts County, Preston North End, Stoke, West Bromwich Albion and Wolverhampton Wanderers.

The first English League Champions were Preston North End, who went through the whole 1888-89 season undefeated. They also won the FA Cup in that year, thus completing the first ever double.

The First English Football League Final Table, Season 1888-89

		P	W	D	L	F	A	Pts
1	Preston North End	22	18	4	0	74	15	40
2	Aston Villa	22	12	5	5	61	43	29
3	Wolverhampton Wanderers	22	12	4	6	50	37	28
4	Blackburn Rovers	22	10	6	6	66	45	26
5	Bolton Wanderers	22	10	2	10	63	59	22
6	West Bromwich Albion	22	10	2	10	40	46	22
7	Accrington	22	6	8	8	48	48	20
8	Everton	22	9	2	11	35	46	20
9	Burnley	22	7	3	12	42	62	17
10	Derby County	22	7	2	13	41	61	16
11	Notts County	22	5	2	15	40	73	12
12	Stoke	22	4	4	14	26	51	12

Preston North End retained the Championship in 1889-90; the runners-up this time were Everton.

Blackburn Rovers beat The Wednesday 6-1 in the 1890 FA Cup Final and William Townley became the first man to score a hat-trick in this fixture.

In 1891-92, the First Division was enlarged to 14 clubs - the two new entrants were Darwen and Stoke.

FA Cup Finals of the 1880s

1880	Clapham Rovers	1	Oxford University	0
1881	Old Carthusians	3	Old Etonians	0
1882	Old Etonians	1	Blackburn Rovers	0
1883	Blackburn Olympic	2	Old Etonians	1(aet)
1884	Blackburn Rovers	2	Queen's Park	1
1885	Blackburn Rovers	2	Queen's Park	0
1886	Blackburn Rovers	0	West Bromwich Albion	0
	Replay			
	Blackburn Rovers	2	West Bromwich Albion	0
1887	Aston Villa	2	West Bromwich Albion	0
1888	West Bromwich Albion	2	Preston North End	1
1889	Preston North End	3	Wolverhampton Wdrs	0

Scottish FA Cup Finals of the 1880s

1880	Queen's Park	3	Thornliebank	0
1881	Queen's Park	3	Dumbarton	0
1882	Queen's Park	4	Dumbarton	2
1883	Dumbarton	2	Vale of Leven	2
	Replay			
	Dumbarton	2	Vale of Leven	1
1884	Queen's Park beat Vale of Leven by default			
1885	Renton	0	Vale of Leven	0
	Replay			
	Renton	3	Vale of Leven	1
1886	Queen's Park	3	Renton	1
1887	Hibernian	2	Dumbarton	1
1888	Renton	6	Cambuslang	1
1889	Third Lanark	2	Celtic	1

The Dawn of Time

On March 15, 1890, England fielded two international sides on the same day - one beat Wales 3-1 at Wrexham, the other beat Ireland 9-1 in Belfast.

In 1890, the Scots followed the English lead and formed their own Football League. The eleven inaugural members were Abercorn, Celtic, Cowlair, Cambuslang, Dumbarton, Heart of Midlothian, Rangers, St Mirren, Renton, Third Lanark and Vale of Leven.

Renton were expelled from the Scottish League after only five matches, for professionalism.

At the end of the season in Spring 1891, there was a tie at the top between Dumbarton and Rangers. In an effort to break the deadlock, a play-off was arranged, but when this ended 2-2 it was decided to share the Championship - the only time this has ever happened.

There was not a single 0-0 draw throughout the whole of the first Scottish League season; 409 goals were scored in 90 matches, an average of 4.5 goals per game.

The First Scottish Football League Final Table, Season 1890-91

		P	W	D	L	F	A	Pts
1=	Dumbarton	18	13	3	2	61	21	29
1=	Rangers	18	13	3	2	58	25	29
3	Celtic	18	11	3	4	48	21	21
4	Cambuslang	18	8	4	6	47	42	20
5	Third Lanark	18	8	3	7	38	39	15
6	Heart of Midlothian	18	6	2	10	31	37	14
7	Abercorn	18	5	2	11	36	47	12
8	St Mirren	18	5	1	2	39	62	11
9	Vale of Leven	18	5	1	12	27	65	11
10	Cowlairs	18	3	4	11	24	50	6

In 1891, the Scots expanded their First Division to 12 clubs.
Cowlairs went out of the League after finishing last in 1891;
the three newcomers were Clyde, Leith Athletic and a
re-formed Renton.

In 1892, the English Second Division was inaugurated. At the end of the
season, there were 'test matches' between the bottom three in Division
One and the top three in Division Two to decide promotion and relegation.

The twelve founder members of the Second Division were
Ardwick, Bootle, Burton Swifts, Burslem Port Vale, Crewe
Alexandra, Darwen, Grimsby Town, Lincoln City, Northwich
Victoria, Sheffield United, Small Heath and Walsall Town Swifts.

The English First Division was increased in size again, from 14 clubs to 16.
The two new additions were Nottingham Forest and The Wednesday.

At the end of the 1892-93 season, Notts County and Accrington
became the first clubs to be relegated from the English First
Division.

At the end of the 1892-93 season, Darwen and Sheffield United became the first clubs to be promoted from the English Second Division.

The top team in Division Two, Small Heath, lost their test match with Newton Heath, the third-from-bottom club in Division One, so neither of these clubs changed divisions the following season.

In 1893, the Scots again followed the English example by recognising professionalism and introducing their own Second Division. The ten clubs that played in it were Abercorn, Clyde, Cowlairs, Greenock Morton, Hibernian, Motherwell, Northern, Partick Thistle, Port Glasgow Athletic and Thistle.

At the end of the 1893-94 season, the English League was expanded from 28 clubs to 31, taking three more clubs into the Second Division.

The three new League members in 1894 were Bury, Leicester Fosse and Manchester City.

The British Ladies' Football Club was formed in 1895 and played its first match at Crouch End, London.

On the night of September 11, 1895, the FA Cup was stolen from the window of football outfitters William Shillcock in Newton Row, Birmingham while it was held by Aston Villa. It was never recovered.

The replacement FA Cup cost Villa £25, and the club were fined as much again by the FA for their negligence in allowing it to be stolen. For several years to come, the winners of the trophy were presented with a replica of the original until a newly designed Cup was specially commissioned in time for the 1911 Final.

English Football League Champions 1888-99

1888-89	Preston North End
1889-90	Preston North End
1890-91	Everton
1891-92	Sunderland
1892-93	Sunderland
1893-94	Aston Villa
1894-95	Sunderland
1895-96	Aston Villa
1896-97	Aston Villa
1897-98	Sheffield United
1898-99	Aston Villa

FA Cup Finals of the 1890s

Year				
1890	Blackburn Rovers	6	The Wednesday	1
1891	Blackburn Rovers	3	Notts County	1
1892	West Bromwich Albion	3	Aston Villa	0
1893	Wolverhampton Wdrs	1	Everton	0
1894	Notts County	4	Bolton Wanderers	1
1895	Aston Villa	1	West Bromwich Albion	0
1896	Sheffield Wednesday	2	Wolverhampton Wdrs	1
1897	Aston Villa	3	Everton	2
1898	Nottingham Forest	3	Derby County	1
1899	Sheffield United	4	Derby County	1

Scottish Football League Champions 1891-99

1890-91	Dumbarton and Rangers
1891-92	Dumbarton
1892-93	Celtic
1893-94	Celtic
1894-95	Heart of Midlothian
1895-96	Celtic
1896-97	Heart of Midlothian
1897-98	Celtic
1898-99	Rangers

Scottish FA Cup Finals of the 1890s

1890	Queen's Park	1	Vale of Leven	1
	Replay			
	Queen's Park	2	Vale of Leven	1
1891	Heart of Midlothian	1	Dumbarton	0
1892	Celtic	5	Queen's Park	1
1893	Queen's Park	2	Celtic	1
1894	Rangers	3	Celtic	1
1895	St Bernard's	2	Renton	1
1896	Heart of Midlothian	3	Hibernian	1
1897	Rangers	5	Dumbarton	1
1898	Rangers	2	Kilmarnock	0
1899	Celtic	2	Rangers	0

In 1898-99, the English Football League was enlarged to 36 clubs by increasing both divisions to 18 clubs. The four new members were Barnsley, Burslem Port Vale, Glossop and New Brighton Tower.

THE EARLY
20TH CENTURY

The first League Champions of the 20th century were Aston Villa - with 77 goals, they were the First Division's leading scorers for the sixth season running.

The first FA Cup winners of the 20th century were Bury - they won it again in 1903, but had no other major honours before the millennium. The attendance at the 1900 Cup Final was 68,945.

The first Scottish League Champions of the 20th century were Rangers.

The first Scottish FA Cup winners of the 20th century were Celtic.

The 1901 Cup Final between Tottenham Hotspur and Sheffield United drew a record crowd of 114,815.

The Sheffield United goalkeeper in the 1900 Final was Willie Foulke, who weighed at least 20 stones throughout his career.

There were numerous legends about Foulke. He was said to have been able to carry a man under each arm and to punch the ball as far as the halfway line. One match in which he played had to be stopped when the crossbar snapped after he swung on it.

Of the bottom five clubs in the First Division at the end of the 1900-01 season, four - Sheffield United, Aston Villa, Preston North End and West Bromwich Albion - had won the Championship, the FA Cup or both.

In 1900-01, Linthous dropped out of the Scottish League but its total membership increased to 21 clubs with the addition of East Stirlingshire and St Bernard's.

Scotland beat England 4-1 in the 1900 Home International Championship match. Three of their goals were scored by R.S. McColl of Queen's Park, the last remaining Scottish amateur.

On February 23, 1901, Scotland notched up their highest score in an international, beating Ireland 11-0.

For the 1901-02 season, the Scottish League was expanded again, this time to 22 clubs, with the addition of Arthurlie.

On April 5, 1902, 26 people were killed and 500 were injured when a new stand collapsed at Ibrox Park, Glasgow during the Scotland v England match.

The match was replayed at Villa Park, Birmingham. This was the first international in which all the players were professionals. The final score was England 2 Scotland 2.

In 1901-02, the maximum wage for professional footballers in England was £4 a week.

In 1901-02, goalscoring in the First Division reached a record low, averaging only 2.75 goals a game.

Pitch markings were changed for the 1902-03 season - henceforth, the goal area would be 20 yards wide and 6 yards deep; there would be a penalty area at 18 yards and a penalty spot 12 yards from the goal line.

The Early 20th Century

The 1902-03 Home International Championship was a three-way tie between England, Scotland and Ireland.

In 1903-04, the Scottish League grew again - this time to 26 clubs, with the addition of Albion Rovers and Ayr Parkhouse.

On May 21, 1904, the world governing body of football was formed at a meeting in Paris between representatives of the football associations of Belgium, Denmark, France, Holland, Spain, Sweden and Switzerland. It was called FIFA (Fédération Internationale de Football Association).

England became a member of FIFA in 1905 and thereafter rapidly took a leading role in its affairs.

The first international in South America, between Argentina and Uruguay for the Lipton Cup, ended in a draw.

In 1906, Daniel Burley Woolfall of the English FA was elected President of FIFA.

On December 5, 1904, Woolwich Arsenal beat a team of French internationals 26-1.

England international Alf Common became the first £1000 transfer when he moved from Sunderland to Middlesbrough.

In 1904, Sheffield FC - the oldest football club then in existence, founded in 1857 - won their first major honour, the FA Amateur Cup.

In 1904-05, Wales notched up their first international victory over Scotland at the 30th attempt, winning 3-1 at Wrexham.

In 1904-05, Rangers and Celtic finished level on points at the top of the Scottish First Division.

Celtic won the title in a play-off, but if either goal average or goal difference had been used, Rangers would have been Champions - they had scored 83 and conceded 28, which was superior by either method of reckoning to Celtic's 68 for and 31 against.

At the start of the 1905-06 season, the English Football League was enlarged to 40 clubs by increasing the two divisions to 20 clubs each. Because of the reorganisation, there was no relegation from Division One this year. The two clubs to benefit from this were Bury and Notts County, who finished in 17th and 18th place respectively in 1905.

Doncaster Rovers failed to gain re-election after finishing bottom of Division Two in 1904-05.

The five new clubs elected for 1905-06 were Chelsea, Hull City, Leeds City, Stockport County and Clapton Orient.

Also in 1905-06, the FA Cup was increased from five rounds to six.

Liverpool won the First Division in 1906, the first time a newly promoted club had gone on to take the title the following season.

In 1905-06, the Scottish League was altered for the fifth time this century. The League was enlarged to 28 clubs - a 16-club First Division and a 12-club Second Division.

The two new clubs admitted to the Scottish Second Division were Cowdenbeath and Vale of Leven.

In 1906-07, the Scottish League was enlarged to 30 clubs - a First Division of 18 clubs and a Second Division of 12. The newcomers were Dumbarton and - back after a two-year absence - Ayr Parkhouse.

In 1907, Celtic became the first Scottish club to win the League and FA Cup double.

Wales won the 1907 Home International Championship - it was their first victory in this competition and the first time it had been won outright by anyone but England or Scotland.

Newcastle United dropped only one point at home in their Championship-winning 1906-07 season.

When Bristol City finished second in the First Division at the end of the 1906-07 season, this was the highest position ever achieved by a southern club.

A crowd of between 110,000 and 130,000 watched the 1-1 draw between Scotland and England on April 4, 1908.

Falkirk became the first club to score more that 100 goals in a League season - but their total of 103 was not enough to bring them the 1908 Championship, which went to Celtic.

In 1908, the first Charity Shield was played in England between League Champions Manchester United and Southern League winners Queen's Park Rangers.

The 1909 Scottish FA Cup was withheld after riots between groups of rival supporters during the final replay between Celtic and Rangers. The second match had finished 1-1 after a 2-2 draw in the first Final, and many fans were disgruntled because they suspected that the results had been rigged so that the two clubs might gain extra revenue.

On December 11, 1909, Vivian Woodward of Tottenham Hotspur became the first player to score a double hat-trick twice when he slotted six for England in an amateur international against Holland. His previous double hat-trick had been for England against France in 1906 - a match in which he had scored eight!

In 1911, a new FA Cup was commissioned at a cost of 50 guineas (£52.50).

The new trophy was made in Bradford and first presented to one of the local teams - Bradford City - when they won the Cup in 1911.

The Final against Newcastle United featured twelve Scotsmen, eight of whom played for Bradford City.

The second FA Cup - a replica of the one that had been stolen in 1895 and never recovered - was presented to Lord Kinnaird to mark his 21st year as President of the FA.

In his playing career, Kinnaird (1847-1923) had played in nine FA Cup Finals and won five winners' medals with The Wanderers and The Old Etonians.

When the 1912 Cup Final became the third in a row to be drawn, the FA decided that, henceforth, there would be extra time in the first Final if it was needed.

After keeping an unaltered format since 1907, Scotland again increased the size of its League. Instead of 30 clubs, there would henceforth be 32, with a First Division of 18 and a Second Division of 14.

The two new clubs that came into the Scottish League as a result of this reorganisation were Dunfermline Athletic and St Johnstone.

In the 1912-13 season, every player who appeared for Morton in the Scottish First Division scored a goal for the club.

In 1913, England lost to Ireland for the first time, suffering a 2-1 defeat in Belfast. Three minutes before full-time, the crowd mistook a free kick for the final whistle and invaded the pitch. The match could not be restarted, but the result stood.

After this historic victory, Ireland went from strength to strength, and the following year (1914) won the Home International Championship outright for the first time.

The 1914 FA Cup Final between Burnley and Liverpool was the first to be watched by a reigning monarch, King George V.

The 1914 FA Cup Final was the last to be played at Crystal Palace - the following year, it was held at Old Trafford, then the Great War intervened. After the end of hostilities, the 1920, 1921 and 1922 Finals were held at Stamford Bridge. And then in 1923 the fixture moved to Wembley.

The Great War began in August 1914. By the next FA Cup Final on April 24, 1915, most of the spectators were in uniform.

The Khaki Cup Final - as the 1915 fixture became known - was a muted affair played at Old Trafford in front of 49,557 spectators.

The Cup was won by Sheffield United, who beat Chelsea 3-0 in the Final. The trophy was presented to the Blades' captain by Lord Derby, who took the opportunity to make a recruiting speech: 'It is now the duty of everyone to join with each other and play a sterner game for England'.

On Easter Monday 1915, in a First Division match at Middlesbrough, Oldham Athletic full-back Billy Cook refused to leave the field when ordered off by referee Mr H. Smith. So the referee himself went off, ending the game 30 minutes early.

After an FA inquiry into this incident, Oldham were fined £350 and Cook was suspended for a year. But the result - a 4-1 Middlesbrough victory - was allowed to stand.

In the Scottish League Division Two, there was a tie at the top between Cowdenbeath, Leith Athletic and St Bernard's, necessitating a three-way play-off. Cowdenbeath won it - beating both the other teams - but none was promoted because only the Scottish First Division went on playing throughout the rest of the First World War.

The Football League and FA Cup programmes in England and Scotland continued after the outbreak of the First World War on August 4, 1914.

This was a matter of great controversy - the Church of England was particularly strong in its condemnation of those who watched football while others were serving their country.

Nevertheless, the decision had been taken in consultation with the War Office, who thought that maintaining a vestige of normality would be good for morale. Football clubs helped the recruitment drive - there was no conscription at first - and it is thought that eventually perhaps as many as half a million new soldiers were enlisted at football grounds.

At first, though, recruiting drives at football grounds were almost farcically unsuccessful. Only one person enlisted at a 1915 Arsenal game, while at a Nottingham Forest match there was no one at all ready to fight.

Yet although few spectators were keen to join up, many of those who earned their living from football were among the first to enlist. The game produced 100,000 recruits in the first four months of the War and FA statistics revealed that only 600 men who worked in football had not volunteered by August 1915.

The willingness of players to join up was used by the War Office in its recruitment drive. Outside Stamford Bridge, advertisement hoardings bore the legend: 'Do you want to be a Chelsea diehard? ... Follow the lead given by your favourite football players'.

Many professionals who enlisted went into the17th Service Batallion of the Middlesex Regiment based at the Richmond Athletic Ground.

The Footballers' Batallion, as it became known, went into action in France in the summer of 1915. Their second-in-command, Major Frank Buckley, was wounded in the shoulder and lung in 1916. He was later manager of Wolverhampton Wanderers during the interwar years.

By the summer of 1915, gates had dwindled because so many men had gone to fight in France. It was decided to suspend the English League and carry on with regional leagues. Matches would be played only on Saturdays and holidays - there were to be no midweek games and no internationals.

In Scotland, the FA Cup was suspended, but the First Division of the League continued throughout the War.

During the First World War, Scottish First Division players were not allowed to make their whole living from football and their earnings from the game were restricted to no more than £2 a week. The remainder of their income had to be from work that helped the war effort.

With no midweek matches, Scottish clubs sometimes had to play two matches a day. On April 15, 1915, Celtic beat Raith Rovers 6-0 in the afternoon. In the evening, they went to Motherwell - who had lost 3-0 to Ayr that afternoon - and won 3-1.

The First World War was a particularly successful period for Celtic, who went 62 matches without defeat from November 13, 1915 to April 21, 1917.

In 1918, Rangers broke Celtic's domination, winning the League Championship by a single point. Controversially, the Gers took full advantage of the temporary transfers that enabled footballing servicemen who found themselves in a new billet to play for the local side if picked. Their 1918 team had guest players from as far away as Sheffield.

In 1915 there was a match fixing scandal. A Football League committee of enquiry discovered that players in the Manchester United v Liverpool match at Easter had bet large sums on a 2-1 win for United at odds of 7-1. Four players from each side were suspended for life.

The players found guilty of match-fixing were Tom Fairfoul, Tommy Miller, Bob Purcell and Jackie Sheldon of Liverpool, Laurence Cook, Sandy Turnbull, Enoch West and Arthur Whalley of Manchester United.

Of the United players found guilty, only West had actually played in the fixed match. He was the only one of the eight who did not have his ban lifted at the end of the First World War.

In 1918 and 1919, the winners of the Lancashire regional league met the winners of the Midlands regional league in a play-off for the Championship Cup, the wartime equivalent of the League Championship.

In 1918, Midlands league winners Leeds City beat Lancashire league winners Stoke 2-1 on aggregate over the two-legged tie.

In the 1919 Championship Cup play-off - after the end of the War, but before normal fixtures could be resumed - Nottingham Forest (Midlands) beat Everton (Lancashire) 1-0 at Goodison Park after a goalless draw at the City Ground.

In the Nottingham Forest goal in that final was Sam Hardy, the England keeper who normally played for Aston Villa but who was permitted under wartime regulations to guest for a club closer to his billet.

Outstanding among the footballers honoured for their bravery in the First World War was Donald Bell, the Bradford full back, who won the Victoria Cross posthumously at the Battle of the Somme.

Steve Bloomer, the Derby and England forward, retired early in 1914 and was unlucky enough to take a coaching job in Berlin. Instead of taking up his post on arrival in the German capital, he was interned for the duration of the War.

Title Winners of the First World War

London Combination

1915-16	Chelsea
1916-17	West Ham United
1917-18	Chelsea
1918-19	Brentford

Lancashire Regional Tournament

1915-16	Manchester City
1916-17	Liverpool
1917-18	Stoke
1918-19	Everton

Midland Regional Tournament

1915-16	Nottingham Forest
1916-17	Leeds City
1917-18	Leeds City
1918-19	Nottingham Forest

Wartime League Championship

1917-18	Leeds City
1918-19	Nottingham Forest

Scottish League Champions

1915-16	Celtic
1916-17	Celtic
1917-18	Rangers
1918-19	Celtic

BETWEEN THE WARS

The First World War ended on November 11, 1918, but it was not until the following season that football got back to normal and the League programme resumed.

The Home Nations - England, Ireland, Scotland and Wales - withdrew from FIFA because they refused to play against Germany. They remained outside the organisation until 1922.

For the 1919-20 season, the English Football League was increased from 40 to 44 clubs in two divisions of 22.

Glossop had dropped out of the League in 1915, while Leeds City were expelled from it in 1919 because of irregularities in payments to players during the First World War.

During the First World War, 35 guests had played for Leeds, including seven internationals. This was not a problem in itself, because it was permitted under wartime rules, but when the club refused to render accounts for the 1917-18 and 1918-19 seasons, the League threw them out.

In the aftermath of the Leeds scandal, four of its directors and two of its former managers were banned for life from involvement in football and were even forbidden to attend matches.

One of Leeds City's former managers was George Cripps; the other was Herbert Chapman.

Thus there were six vacancies in the new postwar English Second Division. These were taken up by Coventry City, Port Vale, Rotherham County, Stoke City, South Shields and West Ham United.

Coventry City had been formed in 1883 by workers at a bicycle factory and originally played under the name Singer's FC.

Port Vale - who replaced Leeds City in mid-season and took their points - had been a League club before. Founded in 1876, from 1884 to 1911 they were known as Burslem Port Vale. They had been founder members of the Second Division in 1892 but failed to win re-election in 1896. Re-elected in 1898, they resigned from the League in 1907 because of financial difficulties.

Port Vale took their name from that of the house in Burslem, Stoke-on-Trent, where the founders first met.

Rotherham County grew out of a previous club called Thornhill United which had been founded in 1878. Neighbouring Rotherham Town had been a member of the League from 1893 to 1896, when they failed to win re-election. After joining the Second Division, Rotherham County amalgamated with Rotherham Town in 1925 to form Rotherham United.

Stoke were founder members of the League in 1888 but went bankrupt in 1908 and had to resign. They reformed as Stoke City in 1919 to fill one of the new vacancies.

West Ham United started as Thames Ironworks FC, a club formed by workers at a shipyard owned by Arnold F. Hills. Renamed in 1900, the club won election to the Football League in 1919 under the management of Syd King.

The reorganisation of the League was not good news for everyone. Tottenham Hotspur were relegated to the Second Division. This might not have upset them, since they finished bottom of the First Division in 1915, had it not been for the fact that Arsenal took their place in Division One despite having finished only fifth in Division Two in 1915.

With 42 matches instead of 38, there were new records aplenty in the 1919-20 League season. West Bromwich Albion scored a record 104 goals in their Championship year, while Tottenham scored 102 goals to win the Second Division.

On March 15, 1920, at the age of 45 years 229 days, Billy Meredith of Manchester City became the oldest player to appear in an international match - for Wales against England.

COME ON MEREDITH!

For the 1919-20 season, the two divisions of the Scottish Football League were amalgamated into one division of 22 clubs.

Rangers won the Scottish Championship, with a record 71 points from their 42 matches. They scored 106 goals.

At the start of the 1920-21 season, there was another reorganisation of the English Football League. The total number of clubs was increased from 44 to 66 clubs by accepting the en bloc application of every member of the Southern League Division One.

All but one of the new clubs went into the newly formed Third Division. The exception was Cardiff City, who went straight into Division Two; to accommodate this, Grimsby Town, last season's bottom League club, were relegated to the Third.

Cardiff City went from strength to strength, winning promotion to the First Division in their first season in the League.

Lincoln City, who finished next to bottom of the Second Division in 1919-20, were not re-elected. Their place in Division Two was taken by Leeds United, a new club with the same ground and infrastructure as Leeds City.

The 21 Founder Members of the Third Division were as follows: Brentford, Brighton and Hove Albion, Bristol Rovers, Crystal Palace, Exeter City, Gillingham, Luton Town, Merthyr Town, Millwall Athletic, Newport County, Northampton Town, Norwich City, Plymouth Argyle, Portsmouth, Queen's Park Rangers, Reading, Southampton, Southend United, Swansea Town, Swindon Town and Watford.

Facts

The new formation was immediately popular - Millwall's first gate was over 25,000, Portsmouth and Queen's Park Rangers had attendances of over 20,000.

At the other end of the scale, the Second Division match between Stockport County and Leicester City on May 7, 1921, was watched by fewer paying spectators than any other game in League history. Stockport were already doomed to relegation; their Edgeley Park ground was closed, so the match was played at Old Trafford, Manchester.

Only 13 people paid to watch the game, which was a 0-0 draw. Nevertheless, this statistic is not as impressive as it is sometimes made to sound - another 2000 fans stayed on after watching Manchester United earlier the same day.

Dumbarton goalkeeper James Williamson died on the night of November 12, 1921, from injuries sustained in a collision with a member of the opposition during his team's match with Rangers.

The 1921-22 season saw a further expansion of the English League from 66 clubs to 86. The 20 newcomers entered a new Third Division which was regionalised into Third Division (North) and Third Division (South).

The 20 clubs that joined the Football League in 1921 were as follows: Aberdare Athletic, Accrington Stanley, Ashington, Barrow, Charlton Athletic, Chesterfield, Crewe Alexandra, Darlington, Durham City, Halifax Town, Hartlepools United, Lincoln City, Nelson, Rochdale, Southport, Stalybridge Celtic, Tranmere Rovers, Walsall, Wigan Borough and Wrexham.

Lincoln City were making a return to League football after having failed to gain re-election in 1920.

Stockport County were relegated from Division Two at the end of the 1920-21 season but went straight back up again the following year as the first Champions of Division Three (North).

The inaugural winners of Division Three (South) were Southampton. They had come second in the year of the old Third Division but, because of the impending reorganisation, only champions Crystal Palace had been promoted.

In Scotland, the experiment with a single division was abandoned and the League re-formed with 42 clubs - a top division of 22 and a second division of 20.

Because of this reorganisation, there was no relegation from the Scottish First Division at the end of the 1920-21 season, thus saving the bottom two clubs, Dumbarton and St Mirren, from the drop.

Some of the 20 clubs in the new Scottish Division Two had previously been members of the League before the disruptions caused by the First World War.

The full list of clubs in Scottish League Division Two (1921-22) was as follows: Alloa Athletic, Arbroath, Armadale, Bathgate, Bo'ness, Broxburn United, Clackmannan, Cowdenbeath, Dundee Hibernians, Dunfermline Athletic, East Fife, East Stirlingshire, Forfar Athletic, Johnstone, King's Park, Lochgelly United, St Bernard's, St Johnstone, Stenhousemuir and Vale of Leven.

At the end of the 1921-22 season, Alloa Athletic were promoted to the First Division as Champions of the Second.

However, during the course of the season the Scottish League had announced plans to alter its formation yet again - the two divisions were to be reduced to 20 teams each.

This meant that three clubs - Dumbarton, Queen's Park and Clydebank - were relegated from the First Division in 1922.

The bottom two clubs in Division Two at the end of 1921-22 had to drop out of the League - the unlucky sides were Dundee Hibernians and Clackmannan.

On April 28, 1923, the English FA Cup Final was held for the first time at Wembley Stadium.

The finalists were Bolton Wanderers, who finished 13th in the First Division, and West Ham United, who were vying for promotion from Division Two.

Bolton won 2-0, but the day is best remembered for the near disaster in the crowd. The official attendance is given as 126,047, but many thousands of others scaled the walls and broke down flimsy barriers to watch the match.

Unofficially, there are thought to have been at least 200,000 and possibly a quarter of a million people in the stadium.

The masses flowed onto the pitch, making play impossible. They were eventually pushed back by the police, notably by PC George Scorey and his white horse, Billy.

Constable Scorey later said: 'We arrived at kick-off time and were given orders to clear the pitch. Clear the pitch indeed! You couldn't see it'.

The match eventually got under way 45 minutes late. The crowd lined the edge of the playing area, making throw-ins and corners unusually hazardous - on several occasions, the ball stayed in play after bouncing off spectators on the line.

The Cup was presented to the winning captain by King George V.

This near disaster was an early warning of the need to control football crowds more closely. The FA acknowledged this by making all subsequent Finals strictly all ticket.

Two days after their Wembley disappointment, West Ham United had the consolation of winning promotion for the first time after only four years in the League.

On Monday, April 30, West Ham went to Hillsborough and beat Sheffield Wednesday 2-0, a win which took them to the top of the Second Division, ahead of both Notts County and Leicester City on goal difference.

On May 5, the last Saturday of the 1922-23 season, West Ham's final game was at home to second-placed County. Leicester, meanwhile, were away to mid-table Bury.

Notts County beat West Ham 1-0 and went up as Second Division Champions, but the Hammers were still promoted as runners-up on goal difference because Bury beat Leicester.

The leading lights of West Ham's promotion campaign were centre forward Vic Watson, goalkeeper Ted Hufton and winger Jimmy Ruffell.

On January 30, 1923, Lord Kinnaird died. A Scottish international and the winner of five English FA Cup-winner's medals with Old Etonians, Kinnaird had been President of the FA for 33 years.

Since the end of the First World War, amateur football clubs had been increasing the frequency with which they used substitutes. This was frowned upon by the game's governing bodies.

In order to resist this trend and ensure that it did not spill over into the professional game, the International Board redrafted the rules specifically to emphasise that only 11 players were permitted in any game unless the match was a friendly and unless the use of substitutes had been agreed by the two captains in advance.

The growth of English football continued into the 1923-24 season. The League was enlarged again to 88 clubs by increasing the Third Division (North) from 20 to 22 clubs - this created four divisions, each of 22 teams.

At the end of 1922-23, both clubs relegated from Division Two went into the Third Division (North) - these were Rotherham County and Wolverhampton Wanderers.

One club - Nelson - was promoted to the Second Division from Division Three (North), which had previously been composed of 20 clubs.

One club - Bristol City - was promoted to the Second Division from Division Three (South).

This might have created a numerical imbalance, but the symmetry was maintained when Stalybridge Celtic dropped out of the Third Division (North) at the end of 1922-23 after only two seasons in the League.

There were consequently three vacancies in the League, which were filled by Bournemouth, Doncaster Rovers and New Brighton.

Bournemouth went into the Third Division (South), filling the vacancy created when Bristol City were promoted and no club was relegated to this division from Division Two.

Bournemouth were destined to remain in the Third Division (South) throughout its existence, until 1958.

Doncaster Rovers and New Brighton went into the Third Division (North). Their arrival, together with the fact that Rotherham County and Wolverhampton Wanderers were relegated from Division Two, maintained the total number of teams in Division Three (North) at 22, despite the demise of Stalybridge Celtic.

Doncaster Rovers had first joined the League as members of the Second Division in 1901. They lost their place in 1903, returned in 1904, then dropped out again in 1905. Their re-entry coincided with their move to a new, permanent home at Belle Vue.

New Brighton lasted in the League until 1951, when they failed to gain re-election; their place was taken by Workington.

The English League Championship of 1923-24 was the closest ever, with Huddersfield Town beating Cardiff City into second place on goal average. (Goal average was calculated by dividing the number of goals scored by the number of goals conceded.)

At the end of the 1923-24 season, the top of the First Division table read as follows:

	P	W	D	L	F	A	Pts
Huddersfield Town	42	23	11	8	60	33	57
Cardiff City	42	22	13	7	61	34	57

This gave Huddersfield a goal average of 1.8181, which was 0.024 superior to that of Cardiff, who finished with a goal average of 1.7941.

At the age of 41 years and 8 months, Walter Hampson became the oldest player ever to appear in an FA Cup Final, helping Newcastle United to a 2-0 victory over Aston Villa.

Earlier in the season, Billy Meredith of Manchester City had become the oldest player to appear in any round of the FA Cup when he played against Newcastle United at the age of 49 years and 8 months.

The manager of Huddersfield Town was Herbert Chapman, the man who had been banned for life after the Leeds City debacle in 1919.

In winning the 1924 Home International Championship, Wales defeated all three other nations in the same season for the first time. They beat Scotland 2-0 in Cardiff, England 2-1 at Blackburn, and Ireland 1-0 in Belfast.

In their one home match, both captains - Fred Keenor of Wales and Jimmy Blair of Scotland - played for the club at whose ground the game was played, Cardiff City.

In the same tournament, England played their first international match at Wembley - they drew 1-1 with Scotland.

At the start of the 1923-24 season, the Scottish League was expanded again. A 16-club Third Division was introduced, and there was to be a two-up, two-down system of promotion and relegation.

The 16 new clubs in Scottish League Division Three were as follows: Arthurlie, Beith, Brechin City, Clackmannan, Dumbarton Harp, Dykehead, East Stirlingshire, Galston, Helensburgh, Mid-Annandale, Montrose, Nithsdale Wanderers, Peebles Rovers, Queen of the South, Royal Albert and Solway Star.

One of the 16, Clackmannan, was making a return to the League after having been forced to drop out at the end of the 1921 season.

At the start of the 1924-25 season, the FA made two important changes to the rules of football. One concerned corners - before now, the ball was not in play until it had been touched by a player other than the one who took the corner kick. But henceforth it would be in play from the moment it left the corner semi-circle and, as a result, it was now for the first time legal to score direct from a corner.

The other change the FA made was to the offside rule (Law 6), which since 1866 had read as follows:

'When a player plays the ball, any player of the same side who at such moment of playing is nearer to his opponents' goal line is out of play and may not touch the ball himself nor in any way interfere with an opponent, or with the play, until the ball has again been played, unless there are at such moment of playing at least three of his opponents nearer their own goal-line'.

The FA's alteration to this rule was simply: 'From the first sentence of Law 6 delete the word "three" and substitute the word "two"'.

The above 16 words changed football for ever. The effects were apparent immediately - in the last season under the old rule, 4700 goals had been scored in the English Football League; in the first season under the new rule, that total increased to 6373.

The first English League player to score directly from a corner was Billy Smith, for Huddersfield Town against Arsenal on October 11, 1924.

In 1925-26, so many clubs in the Scottish Third Division got into financial difficulties that the League was suspended before the completion of the programme. The bottom club, Galston, played only 15 of their 30 scheduled matches and dropped out of the League for ever only two years after having joined it.

After leading Huddersfield Town to two League Championships in 1924 and 1925, Herbert Chapman moved south to manage Arsenal. His legacy to the Yorkshire team was still powerful, however, and they won the League again in 1926 under the managership of Cecil Potter.

Just before he left Huddersfield, Chapman bought outside right Alex Jackson from Aberdeen for £2500. He scored 16 goals in his first season in England, and made many more for centre forward George Brown, who finished the season with 35, a club record.

Chapman quickly laid the foundations of Arsenal's future greatness. He persuaded club chairman Sir Henry Norris to buy inside forward Charlie Buchan from Sunderland.

Although Norris baulked at the asking price for Buchan of £4000, the two clubs made a deal in which the player moved for £2000 plus £100 per goal.

In his first season with Arsenal, Buchan scored exactly 20 goals - 19 in the League and one in the FA Cup, so Sunderland eventually got the amount they had originally asked for.

Norris was a property developer who first became involved with Arsenal in 1910 when they had gone into liquidation. One of his earliest plans for the club was a proposed merger with Fulham. When this failed to happen, he was influential in the club's move from Woolwich to their present home in Islington.

In 1919, when the Football League was expanded, Sir Henry Norris used his money to secure the Arsenal a place in the First Division which strictly they should not have had because they had finished only fifth in the Second Division in 1915.

Sir Henry Norris moved out of football in 1925 after being found guilty of financial irregularities, including the unauthorised use of a chauffeur. His team, by contrast, have never since been out of the First Division or the Premiership - a record.

In 1926, Manchester City became the first club to reach the FA Cup Final and be relegated in the same season.

In 1927, the FA Cup left England for the only time in its history when the trophy was won by Cardiff City. They beat Herbert Chapman's Arsenal 1-0 in the Final.

The year was a Cup double for Cardiff, who also won the Welsh Cup for the fifth time in their history.

On January 22, 1927, the League match between Arsenal and Sheffield United became the first to be broadcast live on radio.

While the BBC commentator described the action, another voice in the background called out numbers which referred to squares in a diagram of a football pitch printed in that week's *Radio Times*. After a goal was scored, the ball would be returned to the centre circle: this was square No 1 on the diagram, and this popularised the expression 'Back to square one'.

In the Home International Championship, England won at Hampden Park for the first time since 1904. Both England's goals were scored by Everton centre forward William Ralph Dean.

Dean was born in Birkenhead in 1907 and joined local club Tranmere Rovers in 1924. He moved to Everton in 1925, but his career was threatened when he fractured his skull in a motorbike accident.

Dean was almost universally known as Dixie because of his dark complexion (Dixieland - the American Deep South - was famous for its black slaves). The player himself hated the name.

In 1927-28, Dean scored 60 goals in 39 games for Everton in their Championship-winning season, a First Division record that has never been beaten.

One of the all-time greats, Dean scored 18 goals in only 16 appearances for England. In his League career, he scored 379 goals in 437 games.

As the table overleaf shows, Dean is the only England international ever to have scored more than a goal a game.

Facts

England's Most Prolific Scorers

	Caps	Goals	Ratio
Dixie Dean	16	18	1.12
Tommy Lawton	23	22	0.96
Stan Mortensen	25	23	0.92
Nat Lofthouse	33	30	0.91
Jimmy Greaves	57	44	0.77
Gary Lineker	80	48	0.60
Geoff Hurst	49	24	0.49
Alan Shearer	38	18	0.47
Bobby Charlton	106	49	0.46
David Platt	62	27	0.43
Tom Finney	76	30	0.39

William Ralph Dean died in 1980 at Goodison Park after watching Everton play Liverpool.

On September 14, 1928, Jimmy McGrory set a Scottish First Division individual scoring record when he netted eight goals in Celtic's 9-0 victory over Dunfermline Athletic.

In 1927-28, Jim Smith of Ayr United in the Scottish Second Division set a British record of 66 goals in a season. This magnificent tally was run up in 38 matches.

Bathgate dropped out of the Scottish Second Division during the 1928-29 season and were not replaced, thus reducing the Scottish League from 40 clubs to 39.

Arthurlie, another Scottish Second Division club, resigned from the League with four matches unplayed. These were against Bo'ness, East Fife, Forfar Athletic and Stenhousemuir.

Despite these troubles in the lower reaches of the League, top-grade Scottish football had never been healthier on the field. In March, the national side came to Wembley and beat England 5-1. Three of their goals were scored by Alex Jackson of Huddersfield Town. At 5 feet 7 inches in height, Jackson was the tallest of a Scottish forward line that also featured 'The Wee Blue Devil', Rangers' Alan Morton.

When Arsenal's Charlie Buchan retired at the end of the 1927-28 season, manager Herbert Chapman moved swiftly and replaced him with David Jack, an inside right whom he bought from Bolton Wanderers for a then British record transfer fee of £10,890.

On August 25, 1928, Arsenal and Chelsea became the first League clubs to wear numbered shirts.

On April 6, 1929, Jock Buchanan of Rangers became the first player to be sent off in a Cup Final as the Gers went down 2-0 to Kilmarnock.

On May 15, England suffered their first ever defeat on foreign soil, losing 4-3 to Spain in Madrid.

Bradford City won Division Three (North), scoring 128 goals in the process, a League record.

The Scottish League was reorganised again, for the 16th time since 1900, this time into two Divisions of 20 clubs each. As there had previously been 19 in the Second Division and Bathgate had resigned during the previous season, this created two vacancies. These were filled by Brechin City and Montrose.

Brechin City had been formed in 1906 through the amalgamation of the Angus clubs Hearts and Harp. Despite the new team's grand name, the town in which it played was - and remains - the smallest place in the British Isles with its own League football team.

The British Isles were not represented at the inaugural World Cup because of a dispute over payments to amateur players to compensate them for the regular earnings they would have lost by playing football for their countries. FIFA demanded that players be paid for what was known as broken time. The home countries claimed that to make such payments would damage the game and in 1928 all four of them withdrew from both FIFA and from the Olympic football competition.

The first World Cup was staged in Uruguay in 1930. Thirteen nations took part: Argentina, Belgium, Bolivia, Brazil, Chile, France, Mexico, Paraguay, Peru, Romania, Uruguay, the USA and Yugoslavia.

Montrose, the other newcomers, were founded in 1879 and later merged with Montrose United. Nicknamed The Gable Endies, Montrose play their home matches at a ground called Links Park.

The first World Cup Final was played in front of 90,000 people at the Centenary Stadium, Montevideo on July 30, 1930. The match was between the hosts, Uruguay, and neighbouring Argentina.

1930 World Cup Final

Uruguay	4	Argentina 2
Dorado, Cea, Iriarte, Castro		*Peucelle, Stabile*

Uruguay: Ballesteros, Nasazzi, Mascheroni, Andrade, Fernandez, Gestido, Dorado, Scarone, Castro, Cea, Iriarte
Argentina: Botasso, Della Torre, Paternoster, J. Evaristo, Monti, Suarez, Peucelle, Varallo, Stabile, Ferreyra, M. Evaristo

At the end of the match, the World Cup was presented to Jose Nasazzi, the captain of Uruguay, by Jules Rimet, a French lawyer who had become President of FIFA in 1921.

Six years after taking over as manager, Herbert Chapman led Arsenal to the League Championship in 1931.

This was Arsenal's first Championship since joining the Football League in 1893.

Arsenal were the first club from south of the River Trent to win the English League Championship.

Herbert Chapman was the first man to manage two different Championship-winning sides.

Jack Lambert set a club scoring record with 38 goals in the season. Arsenal's other big guns were 28-goal Cliff Bastin, Joe Hulme (14 goals), David Jack (31 goals) and Alex James.

Arsenal won the League with a record number of points - 66.

Arsenal scored 127 goals in the 42-game season - a huge number, but one fewer than runners-up Aston Villa.

In the 1930-31 season, Arsenal failed to score in only one match - a 0-0 draw with Huddersfield Town at Highbury on March 7.

Third-placed Sheffield Wednesday also scored over a hundred goals; at the bottom of the table, relegated Manchester United conceded 115.

West Bromwich Albion became the first club to win the FA Cup and gain promotion in the same season. They were runners-up in the Second Division, seven points behind Everton, whom they beat in the semi-final of the Cup. In the Final, they beat Birmingham City 2-1.

On September 5, 1931, Celtic's Scotland international goalkeeper, John ('Jock') Thompson, aged 23, was killed after sustaining a kick in the head when he dived at the feet of Rangers' forward Sam English during the Old Firm clash at Ibrox.

In 1931, Wigan Borough of the Third Division (North) became the first team to resign from the English Football League during the course of a season. They had played only six games, and their record was expunged.

Wigan Athletic were founded in 1932 to replace Borough, but the new club did not gain a place in the Football League until 1978. Their most famous supporter is believed to be former Russian leader Mikhail Gorbachev - this sounds as if it must be apocryphal, but may not be.

Facts

Reigning Champions Arsenal strove to go one better in 1931-32, reaching the Final of the FA Cup and pushing hard near the top of the First Division throughout the season. But they finished the season empty-handed - they were runners-up to Everton in the League and lost the FA Cup Final 2-0 to Newcastle United.

In 1931-32, the Champions of all four divisions of the English Football League - Everton, Wolverhampton Wanderers, Lincoln City and Fulham - all scored more than 100 goals in the season.

The outcome of the 1932 FA Cup Final turned on a controversial refereeing decision. Newcastle's Jimmy Richardson chased the ball to the byline and then centred for Jack Allen to score. But many people - especially the Arsenal defenders - thought the ball had gone out of play before Richardson reached it, and newsreel footage of the match tends to support this view. The match is sometimes known as The Over-the-Line Goal Final.

Everton's Championship victory came in their first season back in the top flight of English football.

The last club to have won the First Division in their first season back was Liverpool in 1906.

In 1932, Motherwell became the first team other than Celtic or Rangers to win the Scottish League Championship since Third Lanark in 1904. They finished five points ahead of second-placed Rangers and scored a record 119 goals in the 38-game season.

Motherwell's leading scorer was centre forward Bill McFadyean, with 52 goals in 34 games.

Sam Weaver of Newcastle United and England became the game's first acknowledged long-throw expert - he could throw the ball a distance of some 30 yards, from the touchline to the middle of the penalty area.

In November 1932, Armadale and Bo'ness were expelled from the Scottish League after being unable to meet match guarantees. They were not replaced, thus reducing the Scottish League to 38 clubs.

On December 7, 1932, Ted Parris of Bradford City became the first black player to be capped by Wales in their 4-1 victory over Northern Ireland at Wrexham. The second was George Berry of Wolverhampton Wanderers, who made his debut against West Germany in 1979.

How are the mighty fallen. Arsenal were beaten 2-0 in the third round of the 1932-33 FA Cup by Third Division Walsall. Although every leading club has suffered a Cup upset at some time in its history, this is the classic case.

The First Division leaders were weakened by a flu epidemic which robbed them of Eddie Hapgood, Bob John and Jack Lambert. In addition, manager Herbert Chapman dropped Joe Hulme.

Walsall's first goal against Arsenal was scored after an hour's play by centre forward Gilbert Alsop, who headed home from a corner. Five minutes later, Bill Sheppard scored the second from the penalty spot. Tommy Black, the defender who committed the foul in the area, was immediately transfer-listed and never played for Arsenal again.

Arsenal did have the consolation of winning the League for the second time in three seasons and the third time since 1931.

The Gunners began the 1934-35 season where they had left off the previous spring, and went on to their fourth Championship. But their season was overshadowed by the untimely death of manager Herbert Chapman, who succumbed to pneumonia on January 6, 1935, after watching the Arsenal Third XI play at Guildford.

The first manager to win the League Championship with two different clubs, Herbert Chapman was perhaps the greatest tactician and shrewdest transfer market dealer in the history of the game. The only other managers whose achievements even stand comparison with his are Brian Clough (Derby County and Nottingham Forest), Kenny Dalglish (Liverpool and Blackburn Rovers), and Alex Ferguson (Aberdeen and Manchester United), who all won League titles with two different British clubs.

Tactically, Chapman is best remembered for his development of the stopper, or centre back, at the heart of the defence as a response to the challenge of the new offside rule. It seems, however, that the ploy was not his idea but that of one of his players, Charlie Buchan, who forcefully suggested that Arsenal's centre half, Jack Butler, should undertake that role. It was first tried out against West Ham United in 1925-26, and Arsenal won the match 4-0.

The son of a Yorkshire coal miner, Herbert Chapman was born in 1875, eight years before Arsenal itself was founded. Although he studied mining engineering at Sheffield Technical College, he did not follow in his father's footsteps. Instead, he played football for Stalybridge Rovers, Rochdale, Grimsby, Swindon, Sheppey United, Worksop, Northampton, Sheffield United, Notts County and Tottenham Hotspur. After two years at White Hart Lane, he moved back to Northampton as player manager before moving to Leeds City and then Huddersfield. His life was not without controversy, but the histories of great men seldom are.

Herbert Chapman's influence was not confined to the pitch. He lobbied tirelessly in other areas, being responsible for (among other things) the name of the local tube station being changed from Gillespie Road to Arsenal; the use of numbers on the players' shirts, rubber studs, all-weather pitches and floodlighting.

The referee of the 1934 FA Cup Final was Hertfordshire schoolteacher Stanley Rous. Later that year, Rous was appointed FA Secretary and from 1961 to 1974 was President of FIFA. The author of the simplified set of 17 Laws under which football is played today, Rous was knighted in 1949.

The 1934 FA Cup was won by Manchester City, who beat Portsmouth 2-1 in the Final through goals from Freddy Tilson.

The other star of the City team was goalkeeper Frank Swift, then aged 19, who was so overcome at the final whistle that he collapsed in his goal as he bent to pick up his gloves and had to be helped up to the Royal Box to receive his medal.

Frank Swift was famous for his agility and his huge hands, which were known as 'the frying pans'. After the Second World War, he went on to become the first goalkeeper to captain England.

When Frank Swift retired, he became a newspaper sports writer. He travelled with Manchester United to watch them play Red Star Belgrade in the quarter finals of the 1958 European Cup and was killed in the Munich air crash on the return journey.

The second World Cup was held in Italy in 1934. The tournament was hijacked by the ruling Fascists, who sought to use it as an instrument of propaganda and a showcase of extreme nationalism. As the Italian delegate to FIFA said, with evident satisfaction: 'Our guests felt the pulsating of the masculine energies of a bursting vitality in this our Mussolini's Italy'.

Sixteen nations took part in the 1934 World Cup finals - Argentina, Austria, Belgium, Brazil, Czechoslovakia, Egypt, France, Germany, Holland, Hungary, Italy, Romania, Spain, Sweden, Switzerland and the USA.

Pressure on officials was intense, and home advantage was more than usually favourable to the host nation. It was therefore no surprise when Italy reached the Final in Rome on June 10, 1934. Their opponents were Czechoslovakia.

The captains of both Italy and Czechoslovakia were goalkeepers.

1934 World Cup Final

Italy	2	Czechoslovakia	1
Orsi, Schiavio		Puc	

(after extra time: score after 90 minutes 1-1)

ITALY: Combi, Monzeglio, Allemandi, Ferraris, Monti, Bertolini, Guaita, Meazza, Schiavio, Ferrari, Orsi
CZECHOSLOVAKIA: Planicka, Zenizek, Ctyroky, Kostalek, Cambal, Krcil, Junek, Svoboda, Sobotka, Nejedly, Puc

The Jules Rimet trophy was presented to Italian captain Combi by Benito Mussolini, the Fascist leader of Italy.

Between the Wars

The international between England and new World Champions Italy on November 14, 1934, was a notoriously bruising encounter which became known as The Battle of Highbury.

After a quiet opening, the Battle of Highbury exploded into aggressive life after Italian captain Lusito Monti - a former Argentine citizen - was forced to leave the field with a broken foot after going into a tackle with Arsenal's Ted Drake.

Monti's teammates thought that this injury had been caused by foul play, and thereafter their challenges became very physical.

Captain Eddie Hapgood was among the wounded Englishmen - his nose was broken by an elbow in the face. The Italians had enormous incentives to win - money, cars and, perhaps most attractive of all, exemption from military service.

Yet, despite missing a penalty, England went three up in 15 minutes, with two goals from Eric Brook - the man who had missed from the spot - and another from Drake. In the second half, Italy came back strongly with two goals from Guiseppe Meazza, who also hit the bar. But there was no further scoring, and England won 3-2.

Hapgood said after the match: 'It was difficult to play like a gentleman when somebody closely resembling an enthusiastic member of the Mafia is wiping his studs down your legs'.

The Battle of Highbury featured seven Arsenal players - a record number of players from one club in an international match.

In the League, Arsenal went from strength to strength despite the death of Herbert Chapman. Under new manager George Allison, they won the Championship in 1935, their third consecutive League title, scoring 115 goals in the process, 42 of them through Ted Drake.

Ellis Rimmer scored in every round of the 1935 FA Cup as his team, Sheffield Wednesday, carried off the trophy, beating West Bromwich Albion 4-2 in the Final.

At the end of the 1935-36 season, Aston Villa and Blackburn Rovers, founder members of the Football League, were relegated from the First Division for the first time in their history.

In 1937, Millwall became the first Third Division club to reach the semi-finals of the English FA Cup. They lost 2-1 to the eventual winners, Sunderland.

On April 24, 1937, the Scottish Cup Final at Hampden Park was watched by a British record crowd of 146,433. Celtic beat Aberdeen 2-1.

A week earlier, 149,547 people had paid to see Scotland lose 3-1 to England at Hampden Park. This remained the record attendance for an international match until the 1950, when 199,854 people attended the World Cup Final between Brazil and Uruguay at the Maracana Stadium, Rio de Janeiro.

At Wembley on May 1, 1937, a relatively sparse crowd of 93,495 saw Sunderland win the FA Cup for the first time in their great history after a 3-1 Final victory over Preston North End.

The scorer of Sunderland's second goal in the 1937 Final was their captain, England international Horatio Stratton ('Raich') Carter (1913-94), thought by many to have been the greatest inside forward of the inter-War years.

The third World Cup was held in France in 1938. FIFA hoped to attract 16 finalists, and although 36 of the 57 FIFA member nations originally entered the competition, only fifteen nations eventually took part - Belgium, Brazil, Cuba, Czechoslovakia, Dutch East Indies, France, Germany, Holland, Hungary, Italy, Norway, Poland, Romania, Sweden and Switzerland.

Of the rest, Argentina withdrew in something like pique after being turned down as hosts. With war in central Europe now imminent, Mexico and the USA withdrew from the competition; Spain, already consumed by civil war, pulled out before the start of the qualifying tournament; Austria qualified and would have taken part in the tournament had it not been for the fact that, by the start of the finals, they had ceased to exist as a nation after Anschluss with Germany. The FAs of England, Ireland, Scotland and Wales were still in dispute with FIFA, so none of the British nations took part.

Because there were only 15 nations participating, Sweden were given a bye in the first round of matches.

The 1938 World Cup Final was played at the Parc des Princes, Paris on June 19 in front of 55,000 people.

The 1938 World Cup Final

Italy	4	Hungary	2
Colaussi (2), Piola (2)	*Titkos, Sarosi*		

ITALY: Olivieri, Foni, Rava, Serantoni, Andreolo, Locatelli, Biavati, Meazza, Piola, Ferrari, Colaussi
HUNGARY: Szabo, Polgar, Biro, Szalay, Lazar, Sas, Vincze, Sarosi, Zsengeller, Titkos

Italy became the first nation to retain the World Cup. They also retained it for longer than anyone else, because the Second World War broke out in September 1939 and the next World Cup was not held until 1950.

Another attendance record was set on January 2, 1939, when 118,567 people gathered at Ibrox to watch Rangers' traditional New Year match against Celtic.

Portsmouth won the 1939 FA Cup, beating bookies' favourites Wolverhampton Wanderers 4-1 in the Final. Although Portsmouth have never won the trophy before or since, they hold the unique distinction of holding it for longer than any other club - the next Cup Final was not played until 1946.

At the start of the 1938-39 season, Arsenal manager George Allison spent a record £14,000 on Wolverhampton Wanderers' Welsh international Bryn Jones.

On November 16, 1938, Willie Hall equalled the England scoring record with five goals in the Home International match against Northern Ireland at Maine Road, Manchester. The final score was England 7 Northern Ireland 0.

On May 13, 1939, England played World Champions Italy in Milan. Although many people feared a repeat of the 1934 Battle of Highbury, this match was relatively pacific, and the teams drew 2-2. Tommy Lawton of Everton scored first for England; Biavati equalised early in the second half. Then centre forward Piola put the Italians ahead when he diverted the ball into the net with his fist - the offence went unnoticed by the referee. After a long period of England pressure, they finally equalised with a goal by Willie Hall of Tottenham Hotspur.

When Britain declared war on Germany on September 3, 1939, Blackpool were top of Division One and Arsenal were in second place. Football was suspended for the duration of the hostilities, and the League did not recommence until the start of the 1946-47 season.

In 1941, an English-language propaganda broadcast by Rome Radio claimed that the Italians had captured Arsenal forward Cliff Bastin and were holding him as a prisoner of war. This attempt to undermine British morale was unsuccessful because it was common knowledge in this country that Bastin had failed his army medical on the grounds of deafness and had never left the country.

Many footballers became army fitness trainers. Some people objected that this was favouritism, and demanded to know why more professional players were not sent into action in the front line. But most ordinary people were delighted to play training matches under the supervision of - and sometimes on the same side as - the great stars they had watched from the terraces before the War.

Among the leading players who became drill instructors during the Second World War were Ted Drake of Arsenal, Sam Bartram of Charlton Athletic and Tommy Lawton of Everton.

POSTWAR
FOOTBALL

The Second World War ended in August 1945. Although the Football League was not ready to restart in full until the 1946-47 season, the FA recommenced the Cup for 1945-46 on a two-leg, home-and-away basis.

The 1946 Cup campaign was marred by the Burnden Park disaster on March 9, when 33 people were crushed to death and more than 500 injured at Bolton Wanderers' sixth round match with Stoke City. The ground was full to its 65,000 capacity, but more than 20,000 other people were milling around outside. Many had turned up in the hope of catching a glimpse of Stoke star Stanley Matthews. They forced their way into the stadium shortly before kick-off, and the weight of the extra people caused a crash barrier to collapse.

In the aftermath of the tragedy, the Moelwyn Hughes Report recommended limitations on the size of crowds and the licensing of football grounds.

The FA Cup semi-final replay at Maine Road, Manchester, between Derby County and Birmingham City was watched by a crowd of 80,407, which remains the record attendance for a British midweek match at any venue other than Wembley.

This match was held in the afternoon, and the huge crowd it attracted alarmed the government who were concerned about the popularity of football leading to absenteeism from work. They quickly passed legislation to ensure that henceforth matches on working days should be evening kick-offs only.

After six years of War, many people were keen to make the best use of their leisure time and football became more popular than ever before. The greatly increased sums that League clubs were taking on the turnstiles were not, however, lead to an increase in the players' wages. This caused discontent and threats of strikes unless pay was increased from its pre-War ceiling of £8 a week. The threat of industrial action got a result of sorts - the players won an increase to £9 a week.

Bolton Wanderers eventually reached the semi-final of the 1946 FA Cup competition, in which they lost 2-0 to Charlton Athletic. The other semi-final was won by Derby County, who beat Birmingham City 5-1 on aggregate.

The 1946 FA Cup Final was held on April 27 at its now traditional Wembley venue. Derby County were favourites, not least because they had been greatly strengthened by the recent purchase of Raich Carter from Sunderland and Peter Doherty from Manchester City. Although they won - handsomely, in the end - they needed extra time and an own goal from Charlton's Herbert Turner to set them on their way.

A minute later, Turner equalised with a deflected goal for Charlton, thus becoming the first man to score for both teams in a Wembley Cup Final.

During the summer, Dynamo Moscow toured Britain. The Russians led a cloistered existence while they were abroad, eating all their meals at the Soviet Embassy in London and insisting that at least one of their matches be refereed by a Russian.

A the start of their first match, against Chelsea at Stamford Bridge, they presented their opponents with bunches of flowers. Then they drew 3-3 with the Londoners in front of 82,000 people.

In their next match, Dynamo Moscow beat Cardiff City 10-1, then returned to the capital for a game against Arsenal, who fielded Stanley Matthews and Stan Mortensen as guests. The match was played at White Hart Lane because Highbury was being rebuilt. In thick fog, the Russians won 4-3.

In their next game, the Russians drew 2-2 with Rangers. They were then slated to play an FA XI at Villa Park but flew home without notice before the kick off.

Jack Stamps might have won the Cup for Derby in normal time, but his goal-bound effort was thwarted when the ball burst after he had kicked it and it was gathered easily by Charlton keeper Sam Bartram.

In extra time, Derby pulled away, with a goal from Doherty and two from Stamps - final score Derby County 4 Charlton Athletic 1.

The 1946 FA Cup was Derby County's first major honour since joining the Football League in 1888.

In Scotland, a new competition was launched in the 1945-46 season to herald the postwar era. However, the League Cup failed at first to attract a great deal of public interest.

The inaugural Scottish League Cup was won by Aberdeen, who beat Rangers 3-2 in the Final at Hampden. Aberdeen also won the FA Cup in the same year, thus becoming the first British club to do the so-called 'new double'.

At the start of the 1946-47 season, the Scottish League was re-formed again, now with 30 teams divided into Division 'A' of 16 and Division 'B' of 14. This was eight fewer teams than had competed in the Scottish League in 1939 - the clubs that had dropped out in the meantime were Brechin City, East Stirlingshire, Edinburgh City, Forfar Athletic, King's Park, Leith Athletic, Montrose and St Bernard's.

The first English Football League Champions of the postwar era were Liverpool - the 1947 title was the fifth in their history.

On October 3, 1946, Len Shackleton scored six goals on his debut for Second Division Newcastle United after his £13,000 transfer from Bradford Park Avenue. Newcastle went on to beat Newport County 13-0, despite missing a penalty in the second minute.

Newport County eventually conceded a total of 133 goals in the 42-match season and were relegated to the Third Division (South).

Charlton Athletic put last year's disappointment behind them by beating Burnley 1-0 in the 1947 FA Cup Fina!.

The winning goal was scored in extra time by Chris Duffy. The other incident of note in the match was that - for the second year running - the ball burst.

Doncaster Rovers had a record-breaking season as they won the Third Division (North) - the most wins (33), the most away wins (18), the most away points (37) and the highest points total (72) while there were two points for a win. They also had the League's leading scorer - Clarrie Jordan, with 42 goals in the season.

In 1946, the FAs of England, Northern Ireland, Scotland and Wales finally rejoined FIFA, from which they had withdrawn in 1928 because of a dispute over broken time. To celebrate their re-entry, the Home Nations played a Rest of Europe XI in an exhibition match in front of a crowd of 135,000 at Hampden Park, Glasgow.

Great Britain won the match 6-1, with three goals from Wilf Mannion, two from Tommy Lawton and one from Billy Steel.

The only player in the Rest of Europe XI with English as his native language was Johnny Carey of Manchester United and Eire.

Facts ⚽

England centre forward Tommy Lawton moved from Everton to Chelsea after the War but never settled at the London club because of a contractual dispute. In 1947, he was sensationally transferred to Third Division Notts County for a record fee of £20,000 plus wing half Bill Dickson.

At the start of the 1947-48 season, the Scottish League was increased from 30 clubs to 32. The two teams added to Division 'B' were Leith Athletic - returning after a season's absence - and newcomers Stirling Albion.

Stirling Albion were founded in 1945 after the demise of King's Park, another club from the same town. King's Park had dropped out of the Scottish League in 1939; thereafter, they had been plagued by accusations of financial mismanagement and had their ground at Forthbank Park destroyed by German bombs during the War. Stirling Albion had a new ground at Annfield Park.

On January 17, 1948, a record First Division crowd of 83,260 watched Manchester United draw 1-1 with Arsenal. The match was played at United's temporary home, Maine Road.

Old Trafford had suffered greater bomb damage in the War than any other Football League ground - the Main Stand and some of the terraces had been destroyed in 1941 by two German bombs and the pitch itself had been scorched by the resulting inferno. The refurbished stadium did not open again until 1949.

On March 27, 1948, a crowd of 143,570 attended the Scottish FA Cup semi-final between Rangers and Hibernian at Hampden Park, Glasgow - this is a British attendance record for a match other than a cup final.

Arsenal won the 1948 Championship, leading the table from start to finish. They conceded only 32 goals (a First Division record) and more than 2,000,000 watched their games. This was their sixth title, bringing them level with Aston Villa and Sunderland.

The 1948 FA Cup was won by Manchester United, who beat Blackpool 4-2 in a classic Wembley Final.

Blackpool's Stan Mortensen scored in every round of the 1947-48 FA Cup, a total of 10 goals.

On May 4, 1949, a plane carrying the Torino team back from a testimonial game in Portugal against Benfica hit the Basilica of Superga, a village outside Turin. Among the 31 people killed in the crash were 18 footballers, including the entire Torino first team who made up most of the Italian national side.

Torino had been the dominant club in Italy throughout the 1940s, with five successive Championships and victory in the 1943 Italian Cup. In 1948, they had beaten Alessandria 10-0, the highest margin of victory in the history of Serie A.

The victims included Leslie Lievesely, their English manager, captain Valentino Mazzola and Ezio Loik.

After the crash, Torino fielded their youth team in the remaining four matches of the season and, as a mark of respect, their opponents fielded their youth teams against them. Torino won all these games and, with them, the Italian Championship.

Facts

In 1948-49, the English League Championship was won for the first time by Portsmouth. Although they had not a single international player, Pompey were a formidable side with an unbeaten home record - in the 1948-49 season, they won 18 and drew three of their 21 matches at Fratton Park.

Portsmouth also had a good Cup run, but lost in the semi-final to unfancied Leicester City of the Second Division.

The 1948 FA Cup went to Wolverhampton Wanderers. They won the Final 3-1 against a Leicester side suffering from the absence through illness of their promising inside right Don Revie.

Wolverhampton Wanderers captain Billy Wright received the FA Cup from Princess Elizabeth.

The architect of the great Wolves sides of the period was their former centre half Stan Cullis, who had taken over as secretary manager in 1948 from Ted Vizard. The 1949 FA Cup was the start of the most successful period in the club's history, other highlights of which included three League Championships in 1954, 1958 and 1959, and a second FA Cup in 1960.

In 1948-49, Rangers became the first Scottish club to do the domestic treble of League Championship, FA Cup and League Cup.

On March 8, 1950, John Charles of Leeds United became Wales' youngest international when he played for them against Northern Ireland at Wrexham at the age of 18 years 71 days.

Portsmouth retained the League title in 1950, but only just. In 1949, they had romped home, five points ahead of runners-up Manchester United. This year, they needed to beat Aston Villa on the last day of the season to make sure. They won 5-1, making Wolverhampton Wanderers only the second team in League history to be denied the title by goal difference (1.95 against 1.55). The other was Cardiff City, who had been edged out by Huddersfield Town in 1924.

1949-50 Top of the First Division Final Table

	P	W	D	L	F	A	Pts
Portsmouth	42	22	9	11	74	38	53
Wolverhampton Wanderers	42	20	13	9	76	49	53

Arsenal won the FA Cup without leaving London - even their semifinal was played at White Hart Lane because their opponents were fellow Londoners Chelsea.

Losing finalists Liverpool also had a local derby in the semi-finals, beating Everton 2-0.

Arsenal won the FA Cup Final 2-0, both goals being scored by Reg Lewis.

In Scotland, Rangers did the double and completed their second hat-trick of FA Cup wins. The only shadow over their season was defeat in the semifinals of the League Cup by East Fife, the eventual winners of the trophy.

On September 21, 1949, the Republic of Ireland played their first international on British soil, beating England 2-0 at Goodison Park. They were captained by Johnny Carey of Manchester United, and their goals were scored by Con Martin of Leeds United from a penalty and Peter Farrell of Everton, who was playing for the visiting team on his home ground.

After a 12-year gap because of the Second World War, the fourth World Cup was staged in Brazil in June and July 1950. Twelve nations took part - Bolivia, Brazil, Chile, England, Italy, Mexico, Paraguay, Spain, Sweden, Switzerland, Uruguay, the USA and Yugoslavia.

Scotland could have gone to the 1950 World Cup finals, too, but declined to take part after losing to England in the Home International in Glasgow. FIFA had promised the Home Nations two places in the finals, but the Scottish FA announced that they would go only as British Champions. They needed just a draw to win the tournament, but lost 1-0 to England, whose goal was scored by Roy Bentley of Chelsea.

After the match, England captain Billy Wright and Scotland captain George Young pleaded with the Scottish FA to reverse their decision, but to no avail.

West Germany were ineligible for the 1950 World Cup because they were not yet members of FIFA.

Scotland's place in the 1950 World Cup finals was offered to Portugal, but they turned it down.

Turkey qualified for the 1950 World Cup finals but then withdrew - their place was offered to France, who accepted and then changed their minds when they learned the proposed itinerary.

India also withdrew from the 1950 World Cup finals because they refused to wear boots.

Because of these withdrawals, the four South American qualifiers - Bolivia, Brazil, Chile and Uruguay - made it through to the finals without playing a match.

It had originally been thought that the finalists would be divided into four groups of four, but it was so late in the day when it became apparent that only 13 countries would be taking part that other arrangements could not be made - this created a lop-sided tournament with two groups of four, one group of three and one group of only two.

The finals began satisfactorily for England, who beat Chile 2-0 in their opening match with goals by Stan Mortensen and Wilf Mannion. There was little warning of the disaster to come.

The next match was one of the great humiliations in England's footballing history - they lost 1-0 to the USA. The winning goal was scored by Haitian-born Larry Gaetjens. Then they lost 1-0 to Spain and failed to progress beyond the group stage.

Instead of a dramatic knockout, the later stages of the 1950 World Cup were a pool of four countries - Brazil, Spain, Sweden and Uruguay. Brazil and Uruguay beat Sweden and Spain and then faced each other in the deciding match - effectively the Final. This was played at the Maracana Stadium, Rio de Janeiro, on July 16, 1950, in front of the largest crowd in football history - 173,830 people paid, but history books record a total attendance of 199,854.

1950 World Cup 'Final'

Brazil	1	Uruguay	2
Friaca		*Schiaffino, Ghiggia*	

BRAZIL: Barbosa, Augusto, Juvenal, Bauer, Danilo, Bogode, Friaca, Zizinho, Ademir, Jair, Chico
URUGUAY: Maspoli, Gonzales, Tejera, Gambetta, Varela, Andrade, Ghiggia, Perez, Miguez, Schiaffino, Moran

At the end of the match, the football World Cup - which had newly been named The Jules Rimet Trophy in honour of the French President of FIFA - was awarded to Obdullo Varela, the captain of champions Uruguay.

For the 1950-51 season, the English League was enlarged to 92 clubs by increasing both the Third Division (North) and the Third Division (South) from 22 to 24 clubs.

The four new clubs thus admitted to the League for the first time were Scunthorpe United and Shrewsbury Town to the Third Division (North) and Colchester United and Gillingham to the Third Division (South).

Scunthorpe United had been founded in 1899. After entering the League, they won the Third Division Championship in 1958. Their best season in the Second Division was 1961-62, when they finished fourth.

Shrewsbury Town had been founded in 1886 and had twice won the Welsh Cup (1891 and 1938). After election to the English League, they went on to win the Third Division Championship in 1979 and 1994, and have since added a further four Welsh Cup victories - 1977, 1979, 1984 and 1985. In the FA Cup, they reached the sixth round in 1979 and 1982.

Colchester United were founded in 1937 as successors to amateur Colchester Town. They lost their League status in 1990, after finishing bottom of the Fourth Division, but returned in 1992 after winning the GM Vauxhall Conference. The greatest moment in the club's history is probably their victory over Leeds United in the fifth round of the FA Cup in 1971. Colchester won 3-2, and had been 3-0 ahead. Seven members of the team that achieved this great result were over 30 years of age, and it was thus that they acquired the nickname 'Grandad's Army'. In the Football League, Colchester United's best position was third in the Third Division (South) in 1956-57.

Gillingham were founded in 1893 in the wake of the success of another local club, the Royal Engineers. They started life as Excelsior, but in 1894 turned professional and changed their name to New Brompton. They took their present name in 1913. They first joined the Third Division in 1920, but dropped out in 1938 before returning in 1950. Their major League honour has been the Fourth Division Championship in 1964 - their run of 52 home matches without defeat was a record which was not broken until 1981, when Liverpool completed a run of 85 home games without defeat. Gillingham's best FA Cup performance came in 1970, when they reached the fifth round.

On November 15, 1950, Leslie Compton of Arsenal became the oldest British player in history to make his international debut when he played for England against Wales at the age of 38 years 2 months.

On December 13, 1950, Scotland lost for the first time at home to foreign opposition when they went down 1-0 to Austria.

On May 27, 1950, Billy Steel of Derby County became the first Scot to be sent off in an international. Scotland lost 4-0 to Austria in Vienna.

A father and son - Alec (39) and David Herd (17) - played in the same Stockport County team as they beat Hartlepool 2-0 on the last day of the 1950-51 season.

Tottenham Hotspur won the League Championship for the first time in the season after they were promoted from Division Two. Among the stars of their team were two great managers of the future - Alf Ramsey at right back and Bill Nicholson at right half.

Newcastle United won the FA Cup, beating Blackpool 2-0 in the Final. Both goals were scored by Jackie Milburn, and the match is often known simply as 'Milburn's Final'. Many commentators believed that the Seasiders lost this match because they were over-reliant on Stan Mortensen, who was the First Division's leading scorer with 30 goals. Other Blackpool stars of the period were Footballer of the Year Harry Johnson and the incomparable Stanley Matthews on the wing.

George Robledo, the maker of Milburn's first goal, had come to England as a refugee following the revolution in his native Chile. He made his name with Barnsley just after the Second World War and then Newcastle bought him and his brother Ted for £26,500. In his career at St James' Park, George scored 91 goals in 164 matches. When they retired, the pair returned to South America.

On September 19, 1951, Arsenal beat Hapoel Tel Aviv (Israel) 6-1 in the first official match under floodlighting since 1878. Floodlights had been built into the West Stand at Highbury in the 1930s on the orders of their great manager Herbert Chapman, but clubs had been banned from using them by the FA, which feared too much money might be spent.

Newcastle United won the FA Cup again in 1952, thus becoming the first club to retain the trophy in the 20th century.

The last club to win the FA Cup for two years in succession had been Blackburn Rovers (1890 and 1891).

Newcastle beat Arsenal 1-0 in the 1952 Final - the winning goal was scored by George Robledo.

George Robledo was also the First Division's leading scorer, with 33 goals in the 1951-52 season.

Arsenal were desperately unfortunate in this match - Ray Daniel played with a plaster cast on his broken wrist, Doug Lishman had a septic cut and Jimmy Logie an internal haemorrhage. During the game, Walley Barnes had to go off with a knee injury after half an hour, reducing the Londoners to 10 men.

Manchester United won the 1952 Championship after finishing second in four seasons out of the five since the end of the Second World War. It was the third League title in their history, but their first since 1911.

England and Austria drew 2-2 at Wembley on November 28, 1951. The visitors scored first through Melchior, who had been set up by Ernst Ocwirk, their great ball-playing centre half who was nicknamed 'Clockwork' by the British press. England equalised through a penalty by Alf Ramsey and took the lead seven minutes from time through Nat Lofthouse. Two minutes later, however, Stojaspal brought the Austrians back level with another penalty for handball.

TICK TOCK
TICK
TOCK
TICK...

On May 25, 1952, England beat Austria 3-2, thanks mainly to Nat Lofthouse, the Bolton Wanderers centre forward. He scored the first goal after 20 minutes, but Huber equalised almost immediately from a penalty after Froggatt had fouled Dienst. England regained their lead through Sewell of Sheffield Wednesday, then Dienst levelled again just before half time. Lofthouse scored the winner at the end of a 50-yard run, then went off injured but returned to help England hang on to their lead. Henceforth, Lofthouse was always popularly known as The Lion of Vienna.

The 1953 English Champions were Arsenal, winning their seventh League title - a record at the time. The race was very tight, and the Gunners only pipped Preston North End on the very last day of the season, when they beat Burnley 3-2 at home.

1952-53 Top of the First Division Final Table

	P	W	D	L	F	A	Pts
Arsenal	42	21	12	9	97	64	54
Preston North End	42	21	12	9	85	60	54

Arsenal and Preston North End were separated only by goal average - 1.51 against 1.41.

On September 24, 1952, Nat Lofthouse scored six goals for the Football League against the League of Ireland at Molineux - a record for this fixture.

On Boxing Day, 1952, Sheffield Wednesday lost 5-4 at home to
West Bromwich Albion and three of their players scored own
goals. The unlucky trio were Vince Kenny, Norman Curtis and
Eddie Gannon.

Sheffield Wednesday centre forward Derek Dooley broke a leg while
challenging the Preston North End goalkeeper in a game on St Valentine's
Day, 1953. The fracture turned gangrenous and had to be amputated.
Dooley had scored 16 goals in 29 matches that season.

In the Scottish FA Cup on February 28, 1953, Celtic's Charlie Tully
put the ball into the net direct from a corner against Falkirk.
When the referee disallowed the goal because there had been
spectators on the pitch, Tully put the ball in almost exactly the
same spot - this time, the goal stood.

The great highlight of the 1952-53 season was the FA Cup Final between
Blackpool and Bolton Wanderers. In the year of the accession of Queen
Elizabeth II, it would probably be remembered as the Coronation Cup Final,
but it is known as the Matthews Final because of the extraordinary
performance of - and the nation's sentimental attachment to - one great
man: Stanley Matthews.

Stanley Matthews had twice finished on the losing side in classic
Cup Finals - in 1948, when Manchester United won and 1951, the
year of Jackie Milburn.

Bolton went 3-1 up after 55 minutes and it looked as if history was about to repeat itself. At the age of 38, it was almost certainly Matthews' last appearance at Wembley. But after 68 minutes Stan Mortensen scored his own and Blackpool's second as Matthews began to show the world why he was called the Wizard of Dribble.

Bolton held on until the last minute of normal time, when Mortensen became the only man to score a hat trick in the Cup Final, equalising from a free kick just outside the area.

In extra time, Matthews went on another run and set up the winner for Perry, who became the only South African to score in the English FA Cup Final. Final score: Blackpool 4 Bolton Wanderers 3.

Stanley Matthews played until 1965, retiring at the age of 50. He played 54 times for England. He was knighted in 1965.

Rangers did the double in Scotland, but it was a close run thing in both competitions. In the FA Cup, they needed a replay to overcome Aberdeen. Three days after securing the Cup, they beat Dundee 3-1 in their penultimate League match - this left them needing at least a draw in their last game at Queen of the South. The Dumfries team led for much of the game, but thanks to a 75th minute equaliser by Willie Waddell, they finished level on points with Hibernian but took the title because of a greatly superior goal average - 2.05 against 1.82. (If the Championship had been decided on goal difference, the Edinburgh team would have won it.)

1953-54 Top of the Scottish Division 'A' Final Table

	P	W	D	L	F	A	Pts
Rangers	30	18	7	5	80	39	43
Hibernian	30	19	5	6	93	51	43

Since Willie Struth took over as manager in 1920, Rangers had won 18 Championships, 10 FA Cups and three League Cups.

In 1953-54, a new force emerged in English football as Wolverhampton Wanderers won the Championship for the first time in their history. Founder members of the Football League and twice winners of the FA Cup in 1893 and 1908, their history had been otherwise unremarkable. The arrival of Stan Cullis as manager in 1948 and the development of the new so-called 'kick and rush' style led Wolves to the pinnacle of achievement. They were English champions again in 1958 and 1959.

Cullis claimed that Wolves were champions of the world, a boast which led, only slightly indirectly, to the inception of the European Cup in 1955-56.

Runners-up in the League were local rivals West Bromwich Albion, who did have the consolation of winning the FA Cup - they beat Preston North End 3-2 in the Final.

On November 25, 1953, England suffered their first ever home defeat by foreign opposition when they lost 6-3 to Hungary at Wembley Stadium.

Hungary were unbeaten in international football since 1950, with 20 wins in 23 games during that period.

The stars of their glorious victory were centre forward Sandor Kocsis, inside left Ferenc Puskas, Nandor Hidegkuti, who played 'in the gap', right half Jozsef Bozsik and goalkeeper Gyula Groscis.

Hidegkuti scored the opening goal for Hungary in the first minute. England equalised after 13 minutes through Sewell of Sheffield Wednesday, but then Hidegkuti scored again and Puskas added two more before Mortensen brought it back to 4-2 at half time. After the break, Bozsik scored and then Hidegkuti completed his hat trick. England's third goal came from an Alf Ramsey penalty.

Puskas was nicknamed The Galloping Major. At club level, he played centre forward for the Budapest club Kispest, which changed its name in 1949 to Honved and won four consecutive League titles. He retired in 1966, after scoring 83 goals in 84 internationals, a record surpassed only by Pele of Brazil.

Kocsis - nicknamed Golden Head - played at home for Ferencvaros and then for Honved. He was masterful in the air and scored 75 goals in 68 international appearances for his country.

Hidegkuti played club football for MTK Budapest. Despite his Wembley hat trick, he was, overall, the least prolific of the trio. Nevertheless, he scored 39 goals in his 68 internationals.

The visit of the so-called Magic Magyars was a watershed in English international football. An even worse defeat was to follow in the return match, when England went to Budapest and were beaten 7-1 on May 23, 1954.

In Scotland, Celtic won the double. Rangers fell back from their pinnacle in 1953 - they were knocked of both the Scottish FA Cup and the League Cup at the semi-final stage and finished fourth in Division 'A'.

Jimmy Delaney became the only man ever to win the FA Cup in England, Scotland and Ireland. He won the 1954 FAI trophy with Derry City, and put the medal in his collection alongside those he had already won with Celtic in 1937 and Manchester United in 1948.

The 1954 World Cup finals were held in Switzerland. The format was changed yet again - this time there were four groups of four, each group containing two seeded countries who would not play each other.

The 16 finalists in the 1954 World Cup were Austria, Belgium, Brazil, Czechoslovakia, England, France, Hungary, Italy, Mexico, Scotland, South Korea, Switzerland, Turkey, Uruguay, West Germany and Yugoslavia.

Hungary were the clearest favourites in the history of the competition - most observers already thought of them as world champions in all but name. And they started off like winners, with beating South Korea 9-0 and West Germany 8-3.

England qualified for the finals by winning the Home International Championship. As in 1950, FIFA again offered a place to the runners-up in this competition and, in a change of their earlier policy, the Scots' FA this time accepted it.

After an unlucky 1-0 defeat by Austria, Scotland were demoralised by the resignation of manager Andy Beattie and proceeded to lose 7-0 to Uruguay.

England qualified from the group stage by drawing 4-4 with Belgium and beating Switzerland 2-0. The other seeds in their group were Italy.

The pick of the quarter finals looked like being the match between the form team Hungary and Brazil. It turned out to be a riot both on and off the pitch. Hungary went 2-0 up in 10 minutes through Hidegkuti and Kocsis. Brazil, afraid of being overwhelmed, resorted to rough play and the Hungarians repaid them in the same currency. Three players - Santos and Tozzo of Brazil and Boszik of Hungary - were sent off, and fighting carried on in the dressing rooms after the final whistle. The match is known as The Battle of Berne.

England lost in the quarter finals, 4-2 to Uruguay. In the other two quarter-finals, Austria beat hosts Switzerland 7-5, after having gone from 3-0 down to 5-3 up in only 10 minutes. West Germany - entering the World Cup for the first time after recognition by FIFA - beat Yugoslavia 2-0.

In the semi-finals, West Germany thrashed Austria 6-1, while Hungary beat Uruguay 4-2 in a classic.

The 1954 World Cup Final was held in front of 60,000 spectators at the Wankdorf Stadium, Berne on July 4, 1954.

Ferenc Puskas - the captain of Hungary - had missed the Battle of Berne and the semi-final through injury, but insisted on playing in the Final. The decision seemed vindicated when he opened the scoring after six minutes. Two minutes later, Czibor made the score Hungary 2 West Germany 0.

But the resilient Germans - under the guidance of Sepp Herberger, their manager since 1936 - hit back with a goal from Morlock and two more from Rahn. Final score: West Germany 3 Hungary 2

The 1954 World Cup Final teams were as follows:
West Germany: Turek, Posipal, Kohlmeyer, Eckel, Liebrich, Mai, Rahn, Morlock, O. Walter, F. Walter, Schaefer
Hungary: Grosics, Buzansky, Lantos, Bozsik, Lorant, Zakarias, Czibor, Kocsis, Hidegkuti, Puskas, Toth.

Although the Hungarian national side had twice humiliated England, at club level the tables were turned when Wolverhampton Wanderers beat Honved of Budapest 3-2 in an exhibition match under floodlights at Molineux in 1954-55. The visitors, orchestrated by Puskas, went two up with goals by Kocsis and Machos, but Wolves hit back after half time through a Hancocks penalty and two from Swinbourne.

It was after this match that Wolves manager Stan Cullis claimed his team were champions of the world and was thus instrumental in the creation of the European Cup the following season.

In 1955, Chelsea won the League Championship for the only time in their history. They were managed by former Arsenal star Ted Drake and are thus sometimes nicknamed Drake's Ducklings.

The inaugural European Cup was held during the 1955-56 season. Although entry into this competition eventually became through winning the domestic League Championship, it was at first by invitation. Chelsea were drawn to play Djurgarden of Sweden but withdrew on the advice of the English Football League, who opposed the European Cup because they feared it would cause fixture congestion.

In the FA Cup Final, Newcastle United beat Manchester City 3-1 with goals from Milburn, Mitchell and Hannah. City were hampered by the loss of right back Jimmy Meadows, who had to go off after 20 minutes with a knee injury. This was the second time a Magpies Cup victory had been aided by their opponents' loss of a player - the 1952 defeat of Arsenal had swung on the departure of Walley Barnes with the same kind of injury.

On February 5, 1955, Tommy Briggs of Blackburn Rovers scored seven goals in the 8-3 defeat of Bristol Rovers - an English Second Division record.

On April 20, 1955, two pairs of brothers played for Wales in the Home International against Northern Ireland in Belfast - John and Mel Charles and Ivor and Len Allchurch. John Charles scored a hat trick in a 3-2 Welsh win.

In the Home International decider on April 2, 1955, England beat Scotland 7-2 at Wembley. This was the Scots' record defeat in this fixture, and mirrored their own record victory by the same score in 1878.

This was England's first win against the old enemy at Wembley since 1934. Dennis Wilshaw of Wolves scored four of their goals, Nat Lofthouse of Bolton another two. The seventh was scored by Manchester City inside right Don Revie.

Another landmark of this match was the debut of Duncan Edwards - at the age of 18 years 183 days, he was the youngest England international of the 20th century.

England's Youngest Full Internationals

James Prinsep	v Scotland	1879	aged 17 years 252 days
Tot Rostron	v Scotland	1881	aged 17 years 311 days
Clem Mitchell	v Wales	1880	aged 18 years 23 days
Duncan Edwards	v Scotland	1955	aged 18 years 183 days
Jimmy Brown	v Wales	1881	aged 18 years 210 days
Arthur Brown	v Wales	1904	aged 18 years 328 days
Rio Ferdinand	v Cameroon	1997	aged 19 years 10 days
Michael Owen	v Chile	1998	aged 18 years 59 days

There were two other England debuts in this match - Ken Armstrong of Chelsea and Jimmy Meadows of Manchester City. Neither player won another cap for his country.

In Scotland, for once the Old Firm won nothing. The League Championship went to Aberdeen, with Celtic three points behind in second place and Rangers in third. Clyde beat Celtic in the Scottish FA Cup in a replay after the first match had been drawn 1-1. The Scottish League Cup was won by Heart of Midlothian, who beat Motherwell 4-2 in the Final.

The Scottish League was reorganised yet again for the 1955-56 season and enlarged from 32 clubs to 37 - 18 in Division 'A' and 19 in Division 'B'.

The five newcomers and returnees were Berwick Rangers, Dumbarton, East Stirlingshire, Montrose and Stranraer.

1956 was Manchester's year. Manchester United won the Championship by a record margin under the two points for a win system, with 11 points more than runners-up Blackpool.

Manchester City won the FA Cup, beating Birmingham City 3-1 in a Final that will always be remembered as the one in which City keeper Bert Trautmann broke his neck but played on.

German-born Trautmann had been held captive in England during the Second World War but settled here afterwards and, despite general anti-German feeling, became one of the country's most popular players. Even before his Cup Final heroics, he had been voted the Football Writers' Player of the Year for 1956.

City were 2-0 up at Wembley and cruising to victory when Trautmann was kicked as he dived at the feet of Birmingham's Peter Murphy. Dazed and reeling, he opted to carry on in goal, and the crowd sang 'For He's A Jolly Good Fellow'. Only after he had collected his winner's medal did he go for an x-ray which revealed an injury that could well have been fatal.

Manchester City's goals were scored by Joe Hayes, Jack Dyson and Bobby Johnstone. Although he did not appear on the scoresheet, another star was Don Revie, who returned to play at centre forward after having been dropped by both club and country .

The first European Cup was won by Real Madrid, who beat Reims 4-3 in the Final in Paris. That the Spanish champions were able to come back from 2-0 down is largely to the credit of their great Argentine-born front man Alfredo di Stefano.

Although Di Stefano was a goalscoring No 9, he was not a centre forward in the accepted sense of the term - he ran the play from area to area. Born in Buenos Aires in 1926, he joined Real in 1953 and won 31 international caps for his adopted country, Spain.

In the absence of English champions Chelsea, Britain's sole representatives in the European Cup were Hibernian. The Scots reached the semi-finals of the competition, where they were knocked out by Reims.

In September 1955, Harold Bell missed a match for Tranmere Rovers after 401 consecutive League appearances for the club - a record.

On September 3, Wolverhampton Wanderers equalled Sunderland's record for the number of goals scored away from home in the First Division when they beat Cardiff City 9-1.

For the only time in its history, the Home International Championship was a four-way tie between England, Northern Ireland, Scotland and Wales. The man who made it happen was Johnny Haynes of Fulham and England, who scored a last-minute equaliser for his country in the final match against Scotland at Hampden Park.

On November 28, 1955, the FA Cup second round replay between Carlisle and Darlington at St James' Park, Newcastle, became the first first class match in England to be played under floodlights.

The first floodlit League match was the First Division game between Portsmouth and Newcastle United at Fratton Park on February 22, 1956.

On December 17, with his team 4-0 up at Highbury, Arsenal left back Dennis Evans mistook a whistle in the crowd for the referee signalling the end of the match. He lashed the ball into his own net to give a final score Arsenal 4 Blackpool 1.

In Scotland, Rangers were the 1956 League Champions, Heart of Midlothian won the FA Cup and Aberdeen the League Cup.

At the start of the 1956-57 season, the Scottish League changed the name of Divisions 'A' and 'B' to the First and Second Divisions, respectively.

The English Football League dropped their opposition to the European Cup, and in 1956-57 Manchester United became England's first entrants into the competition.

Manchester United started well in European competition, defeating Belgian champions Anderlecht 2-0 in the first leg in Brussels and then 10-0 in the second leg, which was played at Maine Road because the floodlights at Old Trafford were not yet ready.

United went on to beat Athletic Bilbao and then reached the semi-final, the first leg of which was their first game under floodlights. They lost this 2-0 and went out 5-3 on aggregate to Real Madrid, the holders, who went on to retain the trophy.

Within less than a week of their elimination, Manchester United clinched the Championship and thus had the consolation of knowing that they would be back in the European Cup the following season. They finished eight points ahead of their nearest challengers, Tottenham Hotspur.

United's 13-man championship-winning squad featured the following: Johnny Berry, Jackie Blanchflower, Roger Byrne (captain), Bobby Charlton, Eddie Colman, Duncan Edwards, Bill Foulkes, Mark Jones, David Pegg, Tommy Taylor, Dennis Viollet , Liam 'Billy' Whelan and Ray Wood (goalkeeper).

Manchester United were close to the double, but fell at the last to Aston Villa, who beat them 2-1 in the FA Cup Final. United lost their goalkeeper, Ray Wood, had to go off after only six minutes after sustaining a fractured cheekbone when challenged by Villa's Peter McParland. He was replaced in goal by centre half Jackie Blanchflower. Wood returned to play on the wing.

Both Villa's goals were scored by Irish international McParland; United's reply came from Tommy Taylor.

The champions of each of the four divisions of the English League - Manchester United, Leicester City, Derby County and Ipswich Town - all scored over 100 goals, the first time this had happened since 1931-32.

1957's FA Cup giantkillers par excellence were Bournemouth and Boscombe Athletic. The Third Division (South) side beat Wolverhampton Wanderers 1-0 at Molineux in the fourth round, courtesy of a goal by Reg Cutler, who had earlier collided with a goalpost - play had to be stopped while the post was mended. In the fifth round they beat Tottenham Hotspur 3-1 and led Manchester United 1-0 in the sixth round before two goals by Johnny Berry put paid to the Cherries' dreams of Wembley.

In Scotland, Rangers won the League Championship for the 29th time outright and the 30th time altogether in their history (the 1890-91 title had been shared with Dumbarton).

The Scottish FA Cup was won by Falkirk for the second time in their history (the other occasion had been in 1913). They had been brought round from the brink of relegation by new manager Reggie Smith.

Celtic won the Scottish League Cup, beating Partick Thistle 3-0 in a replay after the first Final had been drawn 0-0 after extra time.

At four minutes past three on the afternoon of February 6, 1958, the season was overshadowed by the terrible Munich air disaster, in which the cream of the so-called Busby Babes of Manchester United were killed.

United were returning from Yugoslavia, where they had just drawn 3-3 in their European Cup quarter final against Red Star Belgrade. After a refuelling stop en route, the Elizabethan airliner of British European Airways (BEA) made two attempts to take off from Munich airport but each time aborted the attempt at the last minute because of snow.

The pilot made a third effort to take off, reached the point of no return, but failed to get the airborne, probably because of the slush on the runway, although some people have attributed the crash to ice on the wings. The plane ploughed through the airport perimeter fence and split in half; the port wing and part of the tail section hit a house.

Of the 43 passengers, 23 lost their lives. Among the dead were eight Manchester United players - captain Roger Byrne, reserve left back Geoff Bent, right half Eddie Colman, left half Duncan Edwards, centre half Mark Jones, outside left David Pegg, centre forward Tommy Taylor and inside right Billy Whelan.

Another of those killed was the former Manchester City and England goalkeeper Frank Swift, who had been there in his new capacity as a newspaper sports reporter.

Among those seriously injured were manager Matt Busby together with Johnny Berry and Jackie Blanchflower, who never played again. Of those who escaped with relatively minor injuries were Bobby Charlton, Bill Foulkes, Harry Gregg, Ken Morgans and Dennis Viollet.

Despite the tragedy, Manchester United fulfilled their fixture commitments. Although - not surprisingly - they lost the second leg of their match with Red Star, UEFA offered the team a place in Europe the following season. The English FA and Football League, however, banned them from participating on this basis.

Three months later, on May 3, 1958, Manchester United played in the Final of the FA Cup. Four of the Busby Babes had recovered sufficiently to play - Bobby Charlton, Harry Gregg, Bill Foulkes and Dennis Viollet.

Bolton Wanderers beat Manchester United 2-0 at Wembley with goals by Nat Lofthouse. The second was controversial because he charged Harry Gregg into the net after the United goalkeeper had parried a shot.

The 1958 League Championship was won by Wolverhampton Wanderers. This was their second title, the first having come in 1954.

John Charles, the Wales and former Leeds United forward, had an outstanding first season in Italy, where he helped Juventus to the Serie A title and was the leading scorer in the top flight with 28 goals in 34 matches.

In England, the leading scorer in 1957-58 was Bobby Smith of Tottenham Hotspur, with 36 in 42 matches.

In Scotland, Jimmy Murray and Jimmy Wardhaugh, two Heart of Midlothian forwards, were joint top scorers with 28 goals apiece.

On October 19, 1957, Celtic recorded the highest score in any major British final when they beat Rangers 7-1 in the Final of the Scottish League Cup. Their scorers that day were Neil Mochan (2), Sammy Wilson, Billy McPhail (3) and Willie Fernie (penalty).

Clyde won the Scottish FA Cup for the third time in their history - the other Bully Wee years had been 1939 and 1955.

In the Final of the first Inter-Cities Fairs Cup, Barcelona beat London 8-2 on aggregate (2-2 away, 6-0 at home).
The 1958 World Cup finals were held in Sweden. It was the first - and, to date, the only - such tournament for which all four British home nations - England, Northern Ireland, Scotland and Wales - have qualified together.

Wales went to Sweden despite failing to win their qualifying group. This was because so many African and Asian countries had withdrawn rather than face Israel that there had to be a ballot of countries that had come second in their groups. Wales won the poll and then beat Israel at home and away in a play-off.

The 16 countries that took part in the 1958 World Cup finals were as follows: **Argentina, Austria, Brazil, Czechoslovakia, England, France, Hungary, Mexico, Northern Ireland, Paraguay, Scotland, Sweden, the USSR, Wales, West Germany and Yugoslavia.**

At the end of the group stages, Scotland were eliminated after finishing bottom of their group. The other three home countries had to play off for a place in the quarter finals - England lost 1-0 to the USSR, but Northern Ireland beat Czechoslovakia 2-1 and Wales defeated Hungary by the same score.

Both Northern Ireland's goals in the play-off were scored by Peter McParland of Aston Villa.

Wales won thanks to goals by Ivor Allchurch of Swansea Town and Terry Medwin of Tottenham Hotspur.

In the quarter finals, Wales lost 1-0 to Brazil, whose goal was Pele's first in the competition.

Northern Ireland lost 4-0 to France, for whom leading scorer Just Fontaine scored two of his record 13 goals in the World Cup finals.

In the semi-finals, Brazil beat France 5-2 - Pele scored a hat trick. In the other semi-final, hosts Sweden upset highly fancied West Germany 3-1.

The 1958 World Cup Final between Sweden and Brazil was held in front of 49,737 spectators at the Rasunda Stadium, Stockholm on June 29, 1958.

The 1958 World Cup Final teams were as follows:
SWEDEN: Svensson, Bergmark, Axborn, Borjesson, Gustavsson, Parling, Hamrin, Gren, Simonsson, Liedholm, Skoglund
BRAZIL: Gylmar, D. Santos, N. Santos, Zito, Bellini, Orlando, Garrincha, Didi, Vava, Pele, Zagalo

The final score in the 1958 World Cup Final was Sweden 2 Brazil 5.

Vava and Pele both scored twice for Brazil, and the fifth was added by Mario Zagalo. Sweden scored through Liedholm and Simonsson.

In 1958-59, the English Football League was restructured by deregionalising the old Third Divisions North and South. The top teams in each of the old divisions (Scunthorpe United and Brighton and Hove Albion) were promoted to Division Two, while the bottom two teams in the Second Division (Doncaster Rovers and Notts County) were relegated to the new Third Division. The teams that finished between second and eleventh in the old Third Divisions went into the new Division Three, while the 12 teams that finished between 13th and 23rd in the Third Divisions North and South made up the new Division Four.

Wolverhampton Wanderers won their third League title, finishing five points ahead of Manchester United.

Manchester United had begun the long, hard road back to their previous pinnacles after the Munich tragedy. Manager Matt Busby had splashed out in the transfer market, buying England international inside forward Albert Quixall from Second Division Sheffield Wednesday for a British record fee of £45,000.

Nottingham Forest won the FA Cup for the first time in the 20th century - their one previous success had been in 1898.

In the Final, Forest beat Luton Town 2-1 despite being reduced to 10 men after 32 minutes when right winger Roy Dwight - who had previously put his team ahead - was carried off with a broken leg.

Middlesbrough centre forward Brian Clough became the Second Division's leading scorer for the second year running, with 42 goals in the season. It was the third consecutive season in which he averaged a goal a game, and he reached 100 goals in his career quicker than any other player in the history of the game.

Denis Law of Huddersfield Town became Scotland's youngest full international when he played for his country against Wales at the age of 18 years 236 days. He scored in Scotland's 3-0 victory.

Jimmy Greaves was the leading scorer in the English First Division, with 32 goals in the season for Chelsea.

Tottenham Hotspur appointed their former player Bill Nicholson as manager in succession to Jimmy Anderson.

Nicholson's appointment was announced just before Spurs' home game against Everton. As if to celebrate, the team went out and beat Everton 10-4 in the highest-scoring First Division match of the 20th century. Captain and centre forward Bobby Smith scored four, Alf Stokes got two, and there were also contributions from Terry Medwin, George Robb and Tommy Harmer and John Ryden. Jimmy Harris scored a hat-trick for the visitors and Bobby Collins hit their other goal.

In Scotland, the honours were shared by three clubs - Rangers won the League, St Mirren the FA Cup and Heart of Midlothian the League Cup. The leading scorer was Joe Baker of Hibernian, with 25.

Burnley won the 1960 League Championship. They had not led the table until the final whistle on the last day of the campaign. This was their second title, their other success having come in 1921.

Burnley's manager was Harry Potts and among their star players were right half Jimmy Adamson, England right winger John Connelly (20 goals in the season), inside forward Jimmy McIlroy, centre forward Ray Pointer (19 goals), inside forward Jim Robson (18 goals) and 18-year-old left back Alex Elder.

Wolverhampton Wanderers, who finished third, became the first English First Division team to score over 100 goals in three consecutive seasons.

The 1960 FA Cup was won by Wolverhampton Wanderers, who beat Blackburn Rovers 3-0 in the Final through an own goal by Mick McGrath and two from their winger Norman Deeley.

The match is remembered for the abuse and rubbish poured by Blackburn supporters onto the Wolves team when they tried to parade the Cup and for objects thrown at the referee. Ewood Park had been a hotbed of discontent and rumour for some weeks before the Final, and Rovers' Northern Ireland star Derek Dougan had put in a transfer request.

To make the Blackburn fans' humour even worse, their left back Dave Whelan went off after he broke a leg in a tackle early in the match.

Brian Clough scored another 39 times in the League for Second Division Middlesbrough and all the goals in the Football League's 5-0 defeat of the League of Ireland in Belfast.

On Good Friday and Easter Saturday (April 15 and 16) 1960, Cliff Holton of Fourth Division Watford became the first player to score hat-tricks on two successive days - one in the 4-2 defeat of Chester, the other in a 5-0 win over Gateshead.

In Scotland, Heart of Midlothian won both the League and the League Cup, while Rangers won the FA Cup.

For the second season running, Scotland's leading scorer was Joe Baker, with 42 goals for Hibernian.

On August 15, 1959, Ian St John scored a hat-trick in two and a half minutes for Motherwell against Hibernian in the League Cup.

Real Madrid retained the European Cup in 1960, beating Eintracht Frankfurt 7-3 in the Final. This was their fifth victory in the five years of the competition. The match at Hampden Park, Glasgow was watched by a crowd of 127,621.

Facts ⚽

Real Madrid went on to win the first World Club Championship between the winners of the European Cup and the South American Copa Libertadores, beating Penarol of Uruguay 5-1 over two legs.

Barcelona retained the Inter-Cities Fairs Cup, beating Birmingham City 4-1 on aggregate over two legs in the Final.

On July 10, 1960, the USSR became the first winners of the European Nations Cup, beating Yugoslavia 2-1 in the Final in Paris. Among the countries that did not take part in this competition were the Home Nations (England, Northern Ireland, Scotland and Wales) Italy and West Germany. Spain pulled out when drawn against the USSR because of the vehement anti-communism of General Franco's government.

THE SIXTIES

The Sixties began with the launch of a new competition in England - the League Cup. Originally, both the semi-finals and the Final of this competition were on a two-legged basis.

The League Cup took a long time to establish itself, and in the first year five leading clubs - Arsenal, Sheffield Wednesday, Tottenham Hotspur, West Bromwich Albion and Wolverhampton Wanderers - all turned down invitations to take part.

The first winners of the League Cup were Aston Villa, who beat Second Division Rotherham United 3-2 on aggregate in the Final.

Tottenham Hotspur became the first team in the 20th century to win the League and FA Cup double. The feat had previously been achieved only twice - by Preston North End in 1889 and Aston Villa in 1897 - and the consensus had long been that the feat could never be repeated because of the higher level of competition and the greater number of fixtures - in 1897, there had been only 16 teams in the First Division; now there were 22.

But Spurs announced their intention of confounding the sceptics by kicking off the with 11 straight wins in the League. By the end of the season, they had scored 115 goals - the highest total since since Arsenal scored the same number in 1934-35 - and clocked up more wins (31) and more away wins (16) than any other team in First Division history. Spurs also equalled Arsenal's 1931 record number of points (66) under the two-points-for-a-win system.

In the modern age of huge squads, it is remarkable to note how few players Tottenham called on throughout their greatest season. The 12 main contributors to their great triumphs were Bill Brown, Peter Baker, Ron Henry, Danny Blanchflower, Morris Norman, Dave Mackay, Cliff Jones, John White, Bobby Smith, Les Allen, Terry Dyson and Terry Medwin.

Spurs' leading scorers in their double year were Bobby Smith, with 28, and Les Allen with 23.

The First Division's leading scorer was Jimmy Greaves, with 41 goals for 12th-placed Chelsea. At 21, Greaves also became the youngest player to score 100 goals in English League football.

In the FA Cup Final, Spurs' opponents, Leicester City, were reduced to 10 men when their right back Len Chalmers had to go off injured after only 18 minutes. The rest of the team hung on grimly, however - outstanding in goal was a young keeper called Gordon Banks. The deadlock was not broken until midway through the second half when Bobby Smith scored for Spurs. Their second goal was scored by Terry Dyson.

After 12 previous unsuccessful applications, Peterborough United were finally elected to the Football League as replacements for Gateshead. They then won the Fourth Division at a canter, scoring 134 goals - a League record. An amazing 52 of them were scored by centre forward Terry Bly.

A threatened strike by members of the Professional Footballers' Association was called off at the last minute in January 1961 when the Football League abolished the £20-a-week maximum wage and agreed to scrap the standard contract which bound players to a club for life.

The PFA's spokesman and one of the main agitators for fairer terms of employment was Jimmy Hill, then an inside forward at Fulham, who later became chairman of Coventry City and afterwards took over his former club. Today, Hill is best known as a football pundit on BBC Television.

The agreement reached between the League and the PFA also headed off the threat of litigation by George Eastham, now of Arsenal, against his former club, Newcastle United, which he accused of restraint of trade when they refused to sell him. This case eventually dragged on until July 4, 1963.

After the abolition of the maximum wage, footballers' pay rose rapidly. The same season, Johnny Haynes of Fulham and England became the country's first £100-a-week player.

Other players had moved to Italy in search of better wages. Among the most prominent were Joe Baker, who moved from Hibernian to Torino for £73,000; Denis Law, who had gone from Manchester City to Torino for £100,000; and Jimmy Greaves, sold by Chelsea to AC Milan for £80,000.

England won the 1961 Home International Championship with a hundred per cent record, beating Northern Ireland 5-2, Wales 5-1 and then Scotland 9-3 at Wembley on April 15. England's goals in this match were scored by Jimmy Greaves (3), Johnny Haynes (2), Bobby Smith (2), Bobby Robson of West Bromwich Albion and Bryan Douglas of Blackburn Rovers.

In Scotland, Rangers took the League and the League Cup, while Dunfermline Athletic won the FA Cup for the first time.

In the European Cup, Real Madrid finally lost a match after winning the trophy every year since the competition started in 1956. They were knocked put in the first round of the 1960-61 competition by fierce national rivals Barcelona.

Barcelona themselves were eventually beaten in the Final, 3-2 by Benfica, the Champions of Portugal.

English Champions Burnley reached the third round of the European Cup, where they took a 3-1 lead against Hamburg in the home leg at Turf Moor but lost the return in Germany 4-1.

The new competition in Europe was the Cup Winners' Cup. Britain's representatives met in the semi-final, where Rangers beat Wolverhampton Wanderers.

Rangers thus became the first British club to play in a major European final. In the only Cup Winners' Cup Final to be played over two legs, Rangers lost 4-1 on aggregate to Fiorentina of Italy.

Rangers had been greatly strengthened by the purchase from Raith Rovers in 1960 of Jim Baxter, who went on to play 34 times for Scotland.

In the third year of the Inter-Cities Fairs Cup, Birmingham City lost for the second time in the Final, beaten 4-2 on aggregate by Roma.

The 1961 Second Division Championship was won by Ipswich Town, managed by Alf Ramsey. Ramsey had taken over from Scott Duncan in 1955 and guided Ipswich to the Third Division (South) Championship in 1957.

In 1961-62, newly-promoted Ipswich Town won the League Championship in their first ever season in the First Division.

Their leading scorer - and the First Division's - was Ray Crawford, with 33 goals. Ted Phillips chipped in with another 28.

Ray Crawford played twice for England that season, against Northern Ireland and Austria.

Burnley were runners-up in both the League and the FA Cup, losing 3-1 in the Final to the holders, Tottenham Hotspur.

Burnley's leading players were Jimmy Adamson - voted Footballer of the Year 1962 - and Northern Ireland international inside forward Jimmy McIlroy, who had come second in the same Football Writers' poll.

Spurs were bolstered by the signing of Jimmy Greaves from AC Milan, after the former Chelsea forward had spent only a year in Italy. The fee was set at £99,999 because Spurs' manager Bill Nicholson did not want to saddle the player with the tag of 'the world's first £100,000 player'. Greaves started to repay the investment - a British transfer record - with a goal in the FA Cup Final.

Burnley's equaliser in this match - scored by Jimmy Robson - was the 100th goal in a Wembley Cup Final.

Spurs won the 1962 FA Cup Final 3-1. Bobby Smith scored their second and Danny Blanchflower clinched it with a late penalty.

Brian Clough - who had scored 197 goals in his 213 League games for Middlesbrough - moved to Sunderland for £45,000. He scored 29 goals in 34 matches for his new club, who missed promotion from the Second Division by a single point.

At the age of 46, Stanley Matthews left First Division Blackpool and went back to Second Division Stoke City for £2500. The local hero's return to the Potteries trebled home gate receipts.

On November 1, the Italian League beat the Scottish League 2-0 at Hampden Park. Outstanding for the visitors were a Welshman, an Englishman and a Scotsman - John Charles, Gerry Hitchens and Denis Law.

In the second League Cup Final, Second Division Norwich City beat Fourth Division Rochdale 4-0 on aggregate over two legs.

The 1962 Second Division Championship was won by Liverpool, who returned to the top flight for the first time since 1954.

Also promoted at the end of 1961-62 were Leyton Orient, for whom the following season would be their first taste of First Division football.

On March 6, 1962, financially beleaguered Accrington Stanley resigned from the Football League with debts of £60,000 and insufficient assets to continue trading. Their results to date that season were expunged from the Fourth Division record and their place in the League was taken the following season by Oxford United.

Accrington Stanley's record at the time of their demise was as follows:

P	W	D	L	F	A	Pts
33	5	8	20	19	60	18

Accrington were founder members of the League, but they had had a chequered history. They had resigned from the League once before, in 1893, in the wake of accusations that they had paid one of their players. In 1896, they disbanded altogether. They pulled themselves together in the early years of the 20th century, however, and regained League status in 1921. Between the Wars, they regularly attracted crowds of about 20,000 and, in 1955, became one of the first clubs to have a match televised. Also in the 1950s, Accrington Stanley became the first English League club to field a side composed entirely of Scots.

Accrington Stanley's last ever match in the Football League was at Crewe Alexandra, where they lost 4-0.

Peel Park - Accrington Stanley's ground from 1919-1962 - is no more. In 1968, a new Accrington Stanley was founded - their home ground is at Livingstone Road and they play in the Northern Premier League.

In the Fourth Division, Wrexham (who won promotion this year) beat Hartlepools United (who had to apply for re-election) 10-1. Three of the Welsh side's players scored hat-tricks - Ron Barnes, Roy Ambler and Wyn Davies.

Reigning English Champions Tottenham Hotspur reached the semi-final of the 1962 European Cup, going down heroically to the Cup holders Benfica, 4-3 on aggregate.

Benfica went on to retain the European Cup, beating Real Madrid 5-3 in the 1962 Final. Hungarian star Ferenc Puskas scored a first-half hat-trick for the Spaniards, but the Portuguese Champions hit back with two goals from their emerging star, 20-year-old Eusebio.

The 1962 European Cup Winners' Cup Final was held in Glasgow - Atletico Madrid drew 1-1 with Fiorentina. The replay in Stuttgart was won by the Spaniards 3-0.

The 1962 Final of the Inter-Cities Fairs Cup was an all-Spanish affair in which Valencia beat Barcelona 7-3 on aggregate.

Dundee won the Scottish League Championship for the first - and, to date, the only - time in their history. Their team included forward Alan Gilzean and defender Ian Ure, two players destined to go on to greater fame south of the border.

Gilzean was the season's leading scorer in the Scottish First Division, with 24 goals.

Rangers did a Cup double. Their 2-0 FA Cup Final victory over St Mirren was the 16th time they had won the trophy. The League Cup Final went to a replay when they drew 1-1 with Heart of Midlothian. But Rangers won the replay 3-1 to take the new Cup for the fourth time in its history.

Scotland recovered well from the fiasco of the previous year and won the Home International Championship handsomely with maximum points, beating Northern Ireland 6-1, Wales 2-0 and England 2-0. This was England's first defeat at Hampden Park for 25 years.

The 1962 World Cup finals were held in Chile, a country that had not recovered after having been severely damaged by a series of devastating earthquakes in 1960. In fact, Chile was preferred to the other main candidates, Argentina, not despite the natural disasters that had befallen it, but because of them. As Chilean FA President Carlos Dittborn put it: 'We have nothing - that is why we must have the World Cup'.

Sixteen countries took part in the 1962 World Cup finals:
Argentina, Brazil, Bulgaria, Chile, Colombia, Czechoslovakia,
England, Hungary, Italy, Mexico, Spain, Switzerland, Uruguay,
the USSR, West Germany and Yugoslavia.

The 1962 tournament is remembered for all the wrong reasons - four
players were sent off and four more broke limbs in the first eight matches.

**The World Cup organising committee called the 16 national
managers together and warned them not to let things degenerate.
But the next group stage match - between Chile and Italy - was
already charged with enormous ill-feeling, not least because of
disparaging remarks made about conditions in the host country by
Italian pressmen.**

The match had only just begun when Chilean players began spitting at their
Italian opponents. Chile's Leonel Sanchez punched Italy's Humberto Maschio
and broke his nose, an assault seen clearly by most people in the stadium
and millions on television, but missed by the linesman who was standing right
next to the incident.

Just before half time, Mario David of Italy was sent off by English referee Ken Aston for trying to kick Sanchez. This reduced Italy to nine men, and they duly lost the match 2-0. The game is often known as The Battle of Santiago.

The eight teams to qualify for the 1962 World Cup quarter finals were Brazil, Chile, Czechoslovakia, England, Hungary, Uruguay, West Germany and Yugoslavia.

England lost 3-1 to Brazil. The scorers were Garrincha (2) and Vava for Brazil, Gerry Hitchens for England.

In the semi-finals, Brazil beat Chile 4-2 in front of the biggest crowd of the tournament - 76,594 - while Czechoslovakia beat Yugoslavia 3-1 in front of the smallest - 6000.

The star of Brazil's defeat of the host country was again Garrincha, who made one of Vava's two goals and scored twice himself before being sent off for retaliation against kicking, spitting and virtually incessant verbal abuse.

Despite his dismissal, however, FIFA ruled that Garrincha would be permitted to play in the Final, which was held in the National Stadium, Santiago, on June 17, 1962 in front of a crowd of 68,679.

BRAZIL: **Gylmar, D. Santos, N. Santos, Zito, Mauro, Zozimo, Garrincha, Didi, Vava, Amarildo, Zagalo**
CZECHOSLOVAKIA: **Schroif, Tichy, Novak, Pluskal, Popluhar, Masopust, Pospichal, Scherer, Kadraba, Kvasnak, Jelinek**

Czechoslovakia went ahead with a goal by left half Masopust; Amarildo equalised for Brazil, then went ahead in the second half through Zito. In the 77th minute, Vava scored the killer goal after the Czech keeper had dropped an innocuous lob from D. Santos.

There were six leading scorers in the 1962 World Cup finals, each with four goals - Albert (Hungary), Garrincha (Brazil), Ivanov (USSR), Jerkovic (Yugoslavia), Sanchez (Chile) and Vava (Brazil).

This was Brazil's second World Cup triumph, putting them level with Italy and Uruguay on number of trophies won.

At the end of the 1962 World Cup, England manager Walter Winterbottom announced his retirement. He was replaced on May 1, 1963, by the first ever full time manager - Alf Ramsey, who had led Ipswich to the League Championship earlier that year.

During the close season, Denis Law returned to England from Italy, purchased by Manchester United from Torino for £115,000.

Torino also sold Joe Baker, their acquisition from Hibernian, to Arsenal for £70,000.

On August 23, 1962, Fulham's England international Johnny Haynes suffered a serious knee injury in a car accident which caused him to miss the greater part of the following season and brought an end to his England career. Haynes played 56 times for his country between 1955 and 1962 and had been captain since 1960.

Everton won the 1962-63 Championship - their sixth league title altogether, but their first since 1939 - under the management of Harry Catterick.

Everton's leading scorers were captain Roy Vernon, with 24 goals, and centre forward Alex Young, with 22.

Their other outstanding player was Brian Labone. This strong and skilful centre half went on to play 26 times for England between 1963 and 1970, and would almost certainly have won many more caps had he not had Jack Charlton to compete with for his national place.

Everton made two big signings in the early months of 1963 - right winger Alex Scott for £40,000 from Rangers and left half Tony Kay for £60,000 from Sheffield Wednesday. On June 5, Kay won his first England cap in their 8-1 defeat of Switzerland in Basel - he had the world at his feet, but two years later he was in jail.

The First Division's leading scorer was again Jimmy Greaves, who scored 37 goals for second-placed Tottenham Hotspur.

The winter of 1962-63 caused the worst disruption ever to the British football programme. Between December 22 and March 16, there was not one Saturday on which it was possible to play the complete programme of fixtures. On FA Cup third round day, only three of the scheduled 32 fixtures were played, and 14 of them were subsequently postponed at least 10 times. This led to an immense log-jam of fixtures - the third round was not completed until March 11.

Bolton Wanderers went the longest period without a match in the history of the English Football League - 70 days from December 8, 1962 to February 16, 1963.

It was during this big freeze that the pools companies first used the pools panel to predict results.

Tottenham Hotspur became the first British club to win a major European trophy when they beat Atletico Madrid 5-1 in the Cup Winners' Cup Final in Rotterdam. Their scorers on that great night were Jimmy Greaves (2), John White and Terry Dyson (2).

For his first match in charge of England - against France in the away leg of the European Nations' Cup first round - Alf Ramsey brought in only one new face, Ron Henry of Tottenham Hotspur. England lost 5-2 in Paris on February 27.

Manchester United won the FA Cup, beating Leicester City 3-1 in the Final with a goal from Denis Law and two from Alex Herd. This was Leicester City's third disappointment in the FA Cup at Wembley.

Stoke City were Champions of Division Two. Their inspiration throughout the season was Stanley Matthews, still the Wizard of Dribble despite his 48 years.

Birmingham City won the League Cup, beating Aston Villa 3-1 on aggregate in the Final. To date, this is the only major trophy in their history.

In Scotland, Rangers did the double. They finished nine points ahead of second-placed Kilmarnock in the League and beat Celtic 3-0 in the replayed FA Cup Final after the first match had been drawn 1-1.

Rangers' - and Scotland's - leading scorer was Jimmy Millar, with 27 goals.

The Scottish League Cup was won by Heart of Midlothian, who beat Kilmarnock 1-0 in the Final.

AC Milan won the 1963 European Cup, beating the holders, Benfica, 2-1 in the Final at Wembley.

AC Milan then went on to make a bid for the World Club Championship against the holders, Santos of Brazil, whose star player was the great Pele. Both legs were won 4-2 by the home team. This necessitated a play-off, which the Brazilians won 1-0.

Valencia became the second club to retain the Inter-Cities Fairs Cup, beating Dynamo Zagreb 4-1 on aggregate in the Final.

On July 4, 1963, in the High Court of England, sitting in judgment in the case of George Eastham v Newcastle United, Mr Justice Wilberforce ruled that Football League regulations concerning the retention and transfer of professional footballers were 'in unreasonable restraint of trade'.

1963-64 was the hundredth anniversary of the founding of the Football Association. To mark the centenary, an exhibition match was held at Wembley in which England defeated a Rest of the World XI featuring Eusebio, Denis Law, Ferenc Puskas, Alfredo di Stefano and Lev Yashin.

The celebrations were overshadowed by allegations in the Sunday newspaper, *The People*, that three Sheffield Wednesday players - Tony Kay, David 'Bronco' Layne and Peter Swan - had conspired to fix the result of their game at Ipswich Town in December 1962. The case eventually came to trial in January 1965.

Liverpool won the 1964 Championship, two years after being promoted from Division Two. This was their sixth League title and their first under the management of Bill Shankly.

Bill Shankly was born in 1919. His playing career started at Carlisle United and he then moved to Preston North End, where he won an FA Cup winner's medal in 1938, the same year as that in which he won all his five caps for Scotland.

Facts ⚽

Shankly became manager of his old club, Carlisle United, in 1949. He then had spells at Grimsby Town (1951-53), Workington (1953-56) and Huddersfield Town (1956-59) before taking over from Phil Taylor at Liverpool in 1959.

When Shankly arrived at Anfield, Liverpool were a Second Division club, having been relegated in 1954. The new manager built a new-style team around the nucleus of three outstanding players - Roger Hunt, Ian St John and Ron Yeats.

Roger Hunt was a goalscorer, with 245 goals in 401 professional matches. He was especially prolific in Liverpool's promotion year (1961-62), when he scored 42 goals in the season. He went on to win 34 England caps and a World Cup winner's medal.

Ian St John was a centre forward bought by Shankly for £37,500 from Motherwell in 1961. Highlights of his distinguished playing career included the winning goal for Liverpool in the 1965 FA Cup Final and 21 caps for Scotland. He is now a television soccer pundit.

Defender Ron Yeats was bought by Liverpool for £22,000 from Dundee United in 1961. Shankly was especially proud of this purchase, reportedly introducing him to the press with the words: 'He's a colossus - come outside and I'll give you a walk round him'. Yeats played twice for Scotland in 1965-66.

With 35 goals in the season for fourth-placed Tottenham Hotspur, Jimmy Greaves was the First Division's leading scorer for the fourth year out of five.

West Ham United won the FA Cup for the first time in their history, beating Preston North End 3-2 in a thrilling Final at Wembley. The London club were twice behind to goals by Holden and Dawson but they came back through John Sissons and Geoff Hurst and eventually won with a headed goal by Ron Boyce in injury time.

Sissons was only 18 at the time, but even younger was Howard Kendall of Preston who - at 17 years 345 days - became the youngest FA Cup finalist this century (in fact, since 1879).

The Hammers' Final victory came shortly after they had suffered their record defeat - 8-2 at home to Blackburn Rovers.

Leicester City won their first major honour, beating Stoke City 4-3 on aggregate in the League Cup Final.

In only their second season in the Football League, Oxford United became the first Fourth Division club to reach the sixth round of the FA Cup.

On November 20, 1963, England v Northern Ireland was the first match at Wembley to be played under floodlights. Although England won the game 8-3, the Home International title ended up as a three-way tie between both these countries and Scotland.

On April 25, 1964, Jim Fryatt of Bradford Park Avenue scored the fastest goal on record after only four seconds of the game against Tranmere Rovers.

In Scotland, Rangers won the League, the FA Cup and the League Cup. Already the only club to have done the treble (in 1949), Rangers had now done it twice.

Kilmarnock were runners-up in the Scottish First Division for the second year running.

The European Cup stayed in Milan, but moved across town from AC to Inter, who beat Real Madrid 3-1 in the Final in Vienna.

The 1964 Cup-Winners' Cup Final went to a replay for the second time in its four-year history. Sporting Lisbon and MTK Budapest drew 3-3 after extra time in the first match in Brussels, so they reconvened in Antwerp, where the Portuguese side won 1-0.

The Inter-Cities Fairs Cup stayed in Spain, but moved from Valencia to Zaragoza, who beat the holders 2-1 in the Final in Barcelona. In a departure from established tradition, this Final was a one-off match.

On May 24, 1964, more than 318 people were killed and 500 seriously injured in Lima when riots broke out after Peru had an equalising goal disallowed in their Olympic qualifying match against Argentina. Police responded to the initial disturbance by firing into the air above the heads of the spectators, who panicked and caused a stampede.

Stanley Matthews was knighted in the Queen's 1965 New Year's list, the first footballer to be so honoured. Sir Stanley retired on February 6, five days after his 50th birthday. He went out on a winning note - in his final League match, Stoke City beat Fulham 3-1.

Manchester United won the 1965 League Championship on goal average from Leeds United.

1964-65 Top of The First Division Final table

	P	W	D	L	F	A	Pts
Manchester United	42	26	9	7	89	39	61
Leeds United	42	26	9	7	83	39	61

Manchester United's goal average was 2.28; Leeds' was 2.12.

Leeds were also runners-up in the FA Cup, losing 2-1 to Liverpool after extra time in the Final. This was Liverpool's first FA Cup triumph.

The 1964 Final was goalless at full time. Liverpool then scored through Roger Hunt, but Billy Bremner equalised for Leeds. Then, with nine minutes left, Ian St John headed the Liverpool winner.

Following the match-fixing allegations made in *The People* newspaper the previous year, on January 26, 1965, at Nottingham Assizes, 10 professional footballers were sent to prison for periods of between four years and four months.

In April, all 10 men were banned from football for life by the FA.

The most prominent of those convicted were Dick Beattie, Jimmy Gauld, Tony Kay and Peter Swan.

Dick Beattie was a former Celtic and Scotland Under-23 goalkeeper who later played for Portsmouth and Peterborough United.

Jimmy Gauld played inside forward for Charlton Athletic, Everton, Plymouth Argyle, Swindon Town and Mansfield Town. It was he who had 'come clean' to the Sunday newspapers the previous April for £7000. He was sentenced to four years' imprisonment and ordered to pay £5000 costs.

Facts

Tony Kay and Peter Swan were England internationals. Their account of what had happened sounded more like naivete than conspiracy - they had simply put a small bet on Ipswich Town, to win at home against their own club, Sheffield Wednesday. They had in no way sought to throw the game - it was just that their opponents were the reigning League Champions and might have been expected to win an end-of-season game against visitors with little to play for.

At the end of the 1964-65 season, Jimmy Dickinson retired after playing 764 games at wing half for Portsmouth - his only club - in a career that began in 1946. He won two Championship medals, in 1949 and 1950, and played 48 times for England. Dickinson died in 1982 at the age of 57.

On July 21, 1965, John White, the Tottenham Hotspur inside forward, was killed at the age of 27 when he was struck by lightning while playing golf in Enfield, Middlesex. White was a member of the great Spurs double-winning side of 1961 2 and played 22 times for Scotland.

Arthur Rowley retired at the end of the season as player-manager of Shrewsbury Town. Rowley was the most prolific League scorer of all time, with 434 goals in a 619-match career. He scored four goals in 24 games for West Bromwich Albion, 27 goals in 56 games for Fulham, 251 goals in 303 games for Leicester City and 152 goals in 236 games for Shrewsbury Town.

1964 FA Cup winners West Ham United returned to Wembley a year later to beat Munich 1860 in the Final of the European Cup Winners' Cup. Both goals in their 2-0 victory were scored by newcomer Alan Sealey. This was the second time an English club had claimed a major European trophy.

In the 1965 League Cup Final, Chelsea beat the holders, Leicester City, 3-2 on aggregate.

Jimmy Greaves was yet again the First Division's leading scorer, but this time he shared the accolade with Andy McEvoy of Blackburn Rovers, both players finishing with 29 goals.

In Scotland, it was third time lucky for Kilmarnock. After finishing in second place in 1962 and 1963, they finally took their first title by a whisker from Heart of Midlothian.

Scottish First Division 1964-65 Top of the Final Table

	P	W	D	L	F	A	Pts
Kilmarnock	34	22	6	6	62	33	50
Heart of Midlothian	34	22	6	6	90	49	50

The margin of Kilmarnock's dramatic last-day victory was one of the narrowest ever recorded: they needed to win their final game of the season by two clear goals away to Hearts themselves. And that is exactly what they did, edging out the Edinburgh club on goal average - 1.88 to 1.84 - a difference of 0.04.

The leading scorer in the Scottish First Division was Jim Forrest, with 30 goals for fifth-placed Rangers.

Celtic won the Scottish FA Cup, beating Dunfermline Athletic 3-2 in the Final.

Rangers won the Scottish League Cup, beating Celtic 2-1 in the Final.

Internazionale retained the European Cup, beating Benfica 1-0 in the Final in their home city, Milan.

For the second and last time to date, the Final of the Inter Cities Fairs Cup was played as a one-off, rather than over two legs, home and away. In it, Ferencvaros of Hungary beat Juventus of Italy 1-0 in the latter's home city, Turin.

In a change to the rules at the start of 1965-66, every League club was henceforth to be allowed one substitute, who could come on for an injured player. On the first day of the new season, Keith Peacock of Charlton Athletic became the first player to come on in this role.

Liverpool won the 1966 League Championship - their second title in three years and the seventh in their history, the same number as Arsenal.

The First Division's leading scorer was Liverpool's Roger Hunt, with 30 in the season.

On December 4, 1965, at Burnley, Frank Saul became the first Tottenham Hotspur player to be sent off in a League match since October 27, 1928.

Everton won the FA Cup for the third time, beating Sheffield Wednesday 3-2 in the 1966 Final. Wednesday went two up through Jim McCalliog and Dave Ford, but Everton hit back with two goals from 21-year-old Mike Trebilcock. Derek Temple scored the winner.

West Bromwich Albion won the 1966 League Cup, beating West Ham United 5-3 on aggregate in the Final.

On 20 March, 1966, the World Cup was stolen from a glass-fronted cabinet in Central Hall, Westminster, London, where it was being displayed in advance of the summer's finals in England. Shortly after the theft, the lid of the Jules Rimet trophy was sent to FA headquarters with a ransom demand. At the subsequent 'drop' a 47-year-old dock labourer was arrested, but the police failed to recapture the Cup itself. Then, a week after the robbery, David Corbett was walking his dog, Pickles, in Beulah Hill, Norwood, South London, when the black-and-white mongrel stopped to dig up a paper parcel that had been hidden under a bush. When the package was opened, it was found to contain the World Cup.

The Scottish Championship went back into the hands of the Old Firm, with Celtic winning their 21st League title.

Celtic also won the Scottish League Cup, beating Rangers 2-1 in the Final. Rangers' consolation was the FA Cup, which they won with a 1-0 win over Celtic in the Final replay after the first match had ended goalless.

Joint leading scorers in the Scottish First Division were Joe McBride of Celtic and Alex Ferguson of Dunfermline Athletic, both with 31 goals. (This Alex Ferguson is not the future manager of Aberdeen and Manchester United.)

After a six-year gap, Real Madrid recaptured the European Cup, beating Partizan Belgrade 2-1 in the Final in Brussels.

Borussia Dortmund won the Cup Winners' Cup, beating Liverpool 2-1 in the Final in Glasgow.

The Inter-Cities Fairs Cup stayed in Spain in 1966, as Barcelona beat Real Zaragoza 4-3 on aggregate in the Final.

The early rounds of the Inter-Cities Fairs Cup were overshadowed by foul play and controversy. In the first leg of the first round tie between Chelsea and Roma, Eddie McCreadie was sent off for retaliation. In the second leg, the English players were pelted with missiles outside the stadium.

Even worse, in the first round match between Leeds United and Torino, Bobby Collins had his thigh broken when tackled crudely by Poletti.

When Leeds United met Valencia in the third round, police were called onto the pitch to deal with fighting between the players, who were taken off by the referee for a 10-minute cooling-off period.

The 1966 World Cup finals were held in England. The main stadium was, of course, Wembley; other matches were held at Ayresome Park (Middlesbrough's ground), Goodison Park (Everton) and Hillsborough (Sheffield Wednesday).

The 16 countries that took part were as follows: Argentina, Brazil, Bulgaria, Chile, England, France, Hungary, Italy, Mexico, North Korea, Portugal, Spain, Switzerland, Uruguay, the USSR and West Germany.

The opening match of the tournament on July 11 between the hosts, England, and Uruguay, was a goalless draw.

The first goal of the tournament was scored by Pele in the group match between Brazil and Bulgaria. He played little further part in the World Cup, however - he was treated so roughly by the Bulgarian defence that he was not fit for the next game against Hungary. Brazil lost this match 3-1, their first defeat in the World Cup since the so-called Battle of Berne against Hungary in 1954.

Pele returned for the final group match against Portugal. Brazil needed to win to remain in the competition, but Eusebio played brilliantly and the Portuguese defence chopped Pele at every opportunity. Result: Portugal 3 Brazil 1, and the holders were out.

England's first goal of the tournament was scored by Bobby Charlton in their second group match, a 2-0 victory over Mexico.

During England's third group match - a 2-0 victory over France - Manchester United half back Nobby Stiles committed an ugly-looking challenge which, despite not being considered a foul by the match referee, moved the FA council to request the withdrawal of the player from the following match. Manager Alf Ramsey replied that he would pick the team he wanted or resign at once. Stiles kept his place in the side.

The surprise package of the 1966 World Cup finals group stages were North Korea, who eliminated Italy with a 1-0 victory at Ayresome Park. The winning goal was scored by Pak Doo Ik.

The eight teams in the 1966 World Cup quarter final line-up were Argentina, England, Hungary, North Korea, Portugal, Uruguay, the USSR and West Germany.

In their quarter final match, North Korea went 3-0 up against Portugal before four goals from Eusebio - two of them penalties - enabled the European nation to come through 5-3.

Meanwhile, the workmanlike USSR edged past Hungary 2-1.

In England's quarter final match against Argentina, the visiting captain, Antonio Rattin, became the first player to be sent off in a World Cup finals tournament. He carried on arguing for eight minutes after the referee had pointed to the tunnel. England won the match 1-0, thanks to a Hurst header after 77 minutes.

West Germany won their quarter final 4-0 against Uruguay, who had two men sent off.

Both England's goals in their 2-1 semi-final victory over Portugal were scored by Bobby Charlton.

In the other semi-final, West Germany defeated the USSR 2-1.

The 1966 World Cup Final was held at Wembley on July 30, 1966 in front of a crowd of 93,000.

ENGLAND: Banks, Cohen, Wilson, Stiles, J. Charlton, Moore, Ball, Hurst, Hunt, R. Charlton, Peters
WEST GERMANY: Tilkowski, Hottges, Schnellinger, Beckenbauer, Schulz, Weber, Held, Haller, Seeler, Overath, Emmerich

West Germany opened the scoring after 13 minutes through Haller, but Hurst equalised on 19 minutes with a header from Moore's free kick. After 78 minutes, England went took the lead through Peters. The Cup looked like England's, but Weber equalised in the dying seconds of normal time.

In extra time, Ball pulled the ball back to the edge of the six-yard box, where Hurst kicked the ball past the West German keeper and onto the crossbar. Almost everyone has an opinion about what happened next, but no one is sure whether the ball then crossed the line or bounced slightly in front of it. Nevertheless, there were only two people in the world whose opinions on the subject mattered - the Russian linesman, Tofik Bakhramov, and the Swiss referee Gottfried Dienst. The former gave a goal and the latter upheld his decision - 3-2 to England.

In the last minute of extra time, Moore sent a long clearance through to Hurst, who ran alone from the half way line to score a conclusive final goal moments before the final whistle.

Leading scorer in the 1966 World Cup finals was Eusebio, with nine goals for Portugal.

In 1966-67, Manchester United won the League Championship for the seventh time in their history, thus equalling the record jointly held at the time by Arsenal and Liverpool.

The First Division's leading scorer was Ron Davies, with 37 goals for 19th-placed Southampton.

The first all-London FA Cup Final was between Tottenham Hotspur and Chelsea. Spurs won 2-1, with goals from Jimmy Robertson and Frank Saul. Chelsea replied through Bobby Tambling four minutes from the end.

It was Spurs' third FA Cup of the 1960s. None of the 1961 double-winning side remained, and there were only two players from their previous Cup victory in 1962 - Jimmy Greaves and Dave Mackay.

The format of the League Cup Final was changed from a two-legged, home and away affair to a one-off showcase match at Wembley.

On March 4, 1967, a crowd of 97,952 saw Third Division Queen's Park Rangers win the League Cup at Wembley by coming back from two goals down to beat First Division West Bromwich Albion 3-2.

Both West Brom's goals were scored in the first half by ex-QPR winger Clive Clark. Then, after 63 minutes, Roger Morgan put Rangers back into contention and after 75 minutes the Londoners equalised through a solo effort by the mercurial Rodney Marsh. The winner - scored by Mark Lazarus - was controversial because the chance came after QPR centre half Ron Hunt had bundled into West Brom keeper Dick Sheppard.

Despite their League Cup triumph, QPR were not allowed to enter the Inter Cities Fairs Cup because the European competition was open only to members of the First Division.

In the first ever six-figure transfer between British clubs, World Cup winner Alan Ball was transferred from Blackpool to Everton for £110,000.

World Cup winning manager Alf Ramsey was knighted in the 1967 New Year's Honours List.

In addition to winning the 1967 Home International Championship, on April 15, Scotland had the extra thrill of becoming the first team to beat the new world champions England, winning 3-2 at Wembley.

In 1967, the club side that stood head and shoulders above everyone else in the northern hemisphere was Celtic, who made a clean sweep of the European Cup, the Scottish League Championship, the Scottish FA Cup, the Scottish League Cup and the Glasgow Cup.

Celtic became the first British team to win the European Cup, with a 2-1 victory over Inter Milan in the Final in Lisbon.

Inter Milan went a goal up after eight minutes from a Mazzola penalty. Thereafter they sat back and soaked up everything the Scots could throw at them.

Inter Milan were the world's leading exponents of a defensive formation known as *catenaccio* (the Italian for 'door bolt').

The rest of the match was wave after wave of Celtic pressure which was all absorbed by the Inter defence until their attacking left back Tommy Gemmell hit the equaliser from 25 yards out after 63 minutes.

Eight minutes from time, Gemmell again advanced down the left, pushed the ball inside to Bobby Murdoch who drove the ball into the area where Steve Chalmers deflected it into the Italian goal for the winner.

Club chairman Robert Kelly acclaimed the European Cup winners as the greatest Celtic team of all time. They are popularly known as The Lions of Lisbon.

Bobby Murdoch's 1967 European Cup Final winner was Celtic's 200th goal of the season.

Of Celtic's other goals, 111 had come in the Scottish League, which they won finishing three points ahead of second-placed Rangers. Twenty-one of these goals were scored by Scotland's leading marksman, Steve Chalmers.

Scottish Footballer of the Year was Ronnie Simpson, the veteran Celtic goalkeeper.

Rangers were also runners-up to Celtic in the Scottish League Cup Final. The two sides were separated on this occasion by a single goal from Bobby Lennox.

In the Scottish FA Cup, Celtic beat Aberdeen 2-0 in the Final, with two goals from Wallace.

In one of the greatest upsets in Cup history, Rangers had been knocked out of the Scottish FA Cup in the first round by Berwick Rangers. Berwick's goal was scored by Sammy Reid after 32 minutes - thereafter, the Glasgow Rangers were held at bay by Berwick's goalkeeper-manager Jock Wallace.

Although Rangers reached the Final of the Cup Winners' Cup, they lost 1-0 in extra time to Bayern Munich.

In the Final of the Inter Cities Fairs Cup, Dynamo Zagreb beat Leeds United 2-0 on aggregate over two legs.

A new rule was introduced at the start of the 1967-68 season - goalkeepers were restricted to four steps before they had to release the ball.

The season began spectacularly on August 12, when Tottenham Hotspur goalkeeper Pat Jennings scored in the Charity Shield against Manchester United with a punt that bounced on the edge of the opposition penalty area and over the head of United keeper Alex Stepney. The match ended 3-3.

The existing British transfer record - Alan Ball's £110,000 move from Blackpool to Everton the previous year - was broken twice this season. First in January, when Martin Chivers went from Southampton to Tottenham Hotspur for £125,000, and again in June, when Leicester City bough Allan Clarke from Fulham for £150,000.

The League Championship stayed in Manchester, but moved across town from United to City. This was City's second title - they had previously won it in 1937.

Much of the credit for Manchester City's achievement went to manager Joe Mercer, the former Everton, Arsenal and England player who had been lured out of retirement to take the helm at Maine Road in 1965, when the club languished in the wrong half of Division Two.

Within a week of taking over, Mercer signed as coach and assistant manager the former Charlton and West Ham player Malcolm Allison. Under the pair of them City won promotion back to the First Division in 1966.

Among the great Mercer-Allison signings were Colin Bell from Bury for £45,000, Francis Lee from Bolton Wanderers for £60,000 and Mike Summerbee from Swindon Town for £35,000.

Tony Book, the Championship-winning Manchester City captain and right back, had been signed at the age of 29 for £13,500 from Plymouth Argyle.

The joint top scorers in the First Division were George Best of Manchester United and Ron Davies of Southampton, both with 28 goals.

Fulham finished bottom of the First Division and were relegated. Since winning promotion in 1959, they had become the League's perennial escapologists - they never finished higher than 10th in the First Division, and were 20th - one place above the drop - three times, in 1962, 1965 and 1966.

Peterborough United were relegated from the Third Division after having had 19 points deducted for offering illegal bonuses to their players.

West Bromwich Albion won their fifth FA Cup on their record-breaking 10th appearance in the Final, beating Everton 1-0 after extra time through a goal by Jeff Astle, who had scored in every round of that season's competition.

Leeds United won the 1968 League Cup, beating Arsenal 1-0 in the Final at Wembley.

In Scotland, Celtic retained the Championship - indeed, they lost only once in the League all season, a 1-0 defeat by Rangers.

Celtic also kept the League Cup, beating Dundee 5-3 in the Final.

The Scottish FA Cup went to Dunfermline Athletic for the second time in their history. They beat Heart of Midlothian 3-1 in the Final.

At the start of the 1967-68 season, the Scottish League was enlarged from 37 to 38 clubs by the admission of Clydebank.

On entry into the Scottish Second Division, Clydebank took the unusual decision not to have a manager, making do with a coach.

Celtic's bid to win the World Club Championship against Racing Club of Argentina ended in failure and some of the most disgraceful scenes imaginable. The teams had drawn 2-2 over two legs - Celtic winning 1-0 in Glasgow and Racing Club winning 2-1 in Buenos Aires - and so a play-off was held in Montevideo, the capital of Uruguay. Six players - four Scots and two Argentines - were sent off and Racing Club 1-0 with a goal after 57 minutes by Cardenas.

Cardiff City of Division Two had a wonderful run in Europe, to which they gained entry through their 12th victory in the Welsh Cup. They reached the semi-final of the Cup Winners' Cup, beating NAC Breda and Torpedo Moscow on the way. Drawn against SV Hamburg in the semi-final, they drew 1-1 in the away leg but went down 3-2 at home.

Bobby Charlton's 45th international goal in a 3-1 victory over Sweden took him ahead of Jimmy Greaves as England's all-time leading goalscorer.

Ten years after the Munich air crash had destroyed the greater part of a great team, Manchester United emerged at the summit of the game when they became the first English club to win the European Cup. They beat Benfica 4-1 after extra time in the Final at Wembley with two goals by Bobby Charlton and one each from George Best and Brian Kidd, the last named playing on his 19th birthday.

Manchester United manager Matt Busby was knighted in the New Year's Honours List.

AC Milan won the 1968 Cup Winners' Cup, beating SV Hamburg 2-0 in the Final in Rotterdam.

Leeds United won another European trophy for England, beating Ferencvaros 1-0 on aggregate in the Final of the Inter Cities Fairs Cup.

The semi-finals and Final of the 1968 European Nations' Cup were held in Italy.

Italy won the tournament, beating Yugoslavia 2-0 in the Final in Rome. The hosts had been lucky to get this far - they had drawn their semi-final against the USSR 0-0 and had gone through on the toss of a coin.

Earlier in the tournament, Alan Mullery had become the first England player to be sent off in an international match during the 1-0 semi-final defeat by Yugoslavia. The winning goal in this match was scored by Dragan Dzajic.

Leeds United won the English Championship in 1969 for the first time in their history. During the season, they were beaten only twice in the League - a record for any English 22-club division. Their points total - 67- was also a record, surpassing Arsenal's 66 points in 1931.

One record Leeds United did not even threaten to break was for the highest number of goals scored - they netted only 66 times in the entire season.

Most of the Leeds Championship-winning side were home-grown or had been brought to Elland Road by the enviably efficient scouting system set up by manager Don Revie. Among the discoveries were goalkeeper Gary Sprake, the wingers Eddie Gray and Peter Lorimer and the play-anywhere defender Paul Madeley.

The exceptions were Johnny Giles, Mick Jones and Mike O'Grady.

Midfielder Giles had been bought from Manchester United for £35,000 to replace Bobby Collins, who was out with a long-term injury after the previous season's Inter Cities Fairs Cup tie with Torino. Already capped 11 times by the Republic of Ireland, Giles went on to play a total of 59 full international matches.

Mick Jones was an England international centre forward bought from Sheffield United for £100,000.

Mike O'Grady was an England international winger who came from Huddersfield Town for £30,000.

Other great names of the Leeds side were World Cup winning centre half Jack Charlton, Scottish international Billy Bremner and Norman Hunter, who went on to play 28 times for England.

Mick Jones was the Champions' leading scorer, with 14 League goals. Overall top scorer was Jimmy Greaves, with 27 goals for Tottenham Hotspur. This was the sixth time since 1959 that Greaves had been either the leading or joint-leading scorer in the First Division.

Once they had won the title, in June 1969 Leeds sought to consolidate their position by buying striker Allan Clarke from Leicester City for £165,000.

In 1969, Manchester City won the FA Cup for the fourth time, beating Leicester City 1-0 in the Final through a goal by Neil Young. Leicester were also relegated from the First Division.

1968 was the year which started the legend of Tommy Docherty, the man who, by his own account, has 'had more clubs than Jack Nicklaus'. In six weeks between November 6 and December 18, he managed Rotherham, Queen's Park Rangers and Aston Villa.

Fulham were relegated for the second year running after finishing bottom of Division Two.

The rise and fall of Northampton Town was the most spectacular in League history. Promoted from Division Four in 1960, they won the Third Division Championship in 1963. They finished second in Division Two in 1965, and spent the 1965-66 season in the First Division, but they finished in 21st place and were relegated. In 1967, they were next to bottom of Division Two. At the end of 1969, they were relegated back to the Fourth Division - a full tour of the English Football League in less than a decade.

A Third Division team won the League Cup for the second time as Swindon Town beat First Division Arsenal 3-1 after extra time at Wembley. Swindon went ahead after 35 minutes with a goal by Roger Smart. There was then an extended period of Arsenal pressure - resisted heroically by the Swindon defence, especially keeper Peter Downsborough before Arsenal equalised after 86 minutes through Bobby Gould. In extra time, Swindon winger Don Rogers tore Arsenal apart almost singlehandedly and scored two more goals that took the Cup to Wiltshire.

1966 World Cup hat-trick hero Geoff Hurst scored six for his club in West Ham United's record victory - 8-0 against Sunderland in the First Division. The other two goals were also scored by famous international names - Bobby Moore and Trevor Brooking.

In 1969, Matt Busby - Munich air crash survivor and European Cup-winning manager - announced that he would stand down at the end of the season after 23 years as Manchester United manager.

In Scotland, Celtic completed the treble for the second time in three years, winning the League Championship, the FA Cup and the League Cup.

In the FA Cup Final, they beat Rangers 4-0 with goals by Billy McNeill, Bobby Lennox, John Connelly and Steve Chalmers.

By the end of the 1960s, the celebrity of leading footballers was on a par with that of pop stars. In 1969, Manchester United's George Best - who was sometimes described in the press as a fifth Beatle - felt emboldened to go in to the office of his manager Matt Busby and demand that Pat Crerand, Denis Law and - most amazingly - Bobby Charlton be moved on. His request was noted but not acted on.

Back in Scotland, Celtic's margin of victory in the League Cup Final was even more emphatic - 6-2 against Hibernian. Lennox scored a hat-trick and there were further goals from Wallace, Auld and Craig.

The European Cup went to AC Milan, who beat Ajax Amsterdam 4-1 in the Final in Madrid.

The Cup Winners' Cup was won by Slovan Bratislava, who beat Barcelona 3-2 in the Final in Basel.

In the Cup Winners' Cup semi-final, Slovan Bratislava had eliminated Dunfermline Athletic, who had knocked out England's representatives, West Bromwich Albion, in the quarter-final.

Newcastle United won the 1969 Inter-Cities Fairs Cup, beating Ujpest Dozsa 6-2 on aggregate in the two-legged Final.

Despite having finished only 10th in the First Division in 1968, Newcastle qualified for the Fairs Cup because the 'one city, one club' rule then in operation meant that Arsenal, Everton and Tottenham Hotspur - who had all come above them in the League - were barred from entering.

Everton won the First Division Championship in 1970 for the seventh time in their history. They scored 66 points - one fewer than Leeds United's record total the previous season.

The leading scorer in the English First Division was Jeff Astle, with 25 goals for West Bromwich Albion.

In 1970, the FA Cup went to Chelsea for the first time.

Leeds United were runners-up in both the League and the FA Cup in the 1969-70 season.

The FA Cup Final went to a replay for the first time in its Wembley history and the first time ever since 1912.

The first 1970 FA Cup Final was a 2-2 draw - Leeds led twice with goals by Jack Charlton and Mick Jones; Chelsea equalised twice through Peter Houseman and Ian Hutchinson.

In the Cup Final replay at Old Trafford, Leeds again took the lead with another goal by Mick Jones, but Chelsea levelled the match after 78 minutes through a Peter Osgood header. Chelsea's winner came just before half-time in extra time, when a long throw by Hutchinson into the Leeds penalty area was headed in. The scorer was defender David Webb, who had been roasted by Eddie Gray in the first match at Wembley.

In the fifth round of the FA Cup, George Best equalled what was then the competition scoring record with six goals for Manchester United as they beat Fourth Division Northampton Town 8-2.

The League Cup was won by Manchester City, who beat West Bromwich Albion 2-1 in the Final.

1970 was a great double year for the blue half of Manchester as City also won the Cup Winners' Cup, beating Gornik Zabrze of Poland 2-1 in the Final in Vienna.

Celtic beat Leeds United 3-1 on aggregate in the semi-final of the European Cup. The Scots won the first leg at Elland Road with a single goal scored after only a minute and a half by George Connelly. Leeds' captain Billy Bremner opened the scoring in the return at Hampden Park to level the tie, but in the second half a goal from John 'Yogi' Hughes restored Celtic's lead. Then Leeds' goalkeeper Gary Sprake had to go off injured; the first time his replacement, David Harvey, touched the ball was to pick it out of the net after a third goal by Bobby Murdoch.

In the European Cup Final in Milan, Celtic lost 2-1 to Feyenoord of Holland after extra time despite having taken the lead through Tommy Gemmell.

Back in Scotland, however, Celtic were still the team to beat, though few did. They won the League Championship for the 25th time in their history and the League Cup for the fifth time in a row, beating St Johnstone 1-0 in the Final.

Celtic were denied another treble by Aberdeen, who beat them 3-1 in the Final of the Scottish FA Cup.

Aberdeen - who had finished second in the League - had not won the Scottish FA Cup since 1947. Their goals in the Final were scored by Joe Harper from the penalty spot and two from Derek McKay. Celtic's goal was scored by Bobby Lennox.

In 1970, Arsenal won their first trophy since the League Championship in 1953 when they beat Anderlecht of Belgium 4-3 on aggregate in the Final of the Inter-Cities Fairs Cup.

The Home International Championship was a three-way tie between England, Scotland and Wales. The England v Northern Ireland match was Bobby Charlton's 100th international cap. The Scotland v England match at Hampden Park on April 25, 1970, was the first 0-0 draw since the inaugural meeting of the old enemies in 1872.

Two founder members of the Football League - Aston Villa and Preston North End - were relegated to the Third Division for the first time in their history.

Bradford Park Avenue failed to gain re-election after finishing bottom of the Fourth Division. Their place in the League was taken by Cambridge United.

Martin Peters moved from West Ham United to Tottenham Hotspur for a British record fee of £200,000. Part of the amount was made up with the transfer in the opposite direction of the once-great Jimmy Greaves, now a victim of alcoholism and - as a player, at least - a mere shadow of his former self.

In the build-up to the 1970 World Cup, El Salvador and Honduras fought a four-day war which was at least partly sparked by animosity generated between the two countries when they met in the qualifying tournament.

The 1970 World Cup finals were held in Mexico. The choice of venue was controversial - the 1968 Olympic Games had been held here and many of the competing athletes had experienced severe problems with the intense heat and the altitude.

During a pre-tournament acclimatisation tour of South America, England captain Bobby Moore was arrested in Bogota and charged with stealing an emerald bracelet worth £600 from a hotel jewellery shop in the Colombian capital.

Moore was placed under house arrest while the rest of the squad went off to beat Ecuador 2-0 in Quito. When they came back to Colombia, the charges were dropped and Moore was exonerated.

Later, the whole incident was convincingly shown to have been an attempt to frame the England captain. Bobby Moore himself remarked: 'The fact that they accused Bobby Charlton of sheltering me while I stole a bracelet proves I'm innocent. Bobby has never done a dishonest thing in his life'.

The 16 finalists in the 1970 World Cup were Belgium, Brazil, Bulgaria, Czechoslovakia, El Salvador, England, Israel, Italy, Mexico, Morocco, Peru, Romania, Sweden, Uruguay, the USSR and West Germany.

Holders England were drawn in the same group as Brazil, Czechoslovakia and Romania. Their matches were played in Guadalajara, where the altitude was lower than in Mexico City but where the daytime temperatures typically reached close to 100°F.

The first of many great matches in this World Cup was the meeting between England and Brazil. England lost 1-0 to a goal by Jairzinho, but the match is best remembered for the save Gordon Banks made from a header by Pele.

The last eight in the 1970 World Cup were Brazil, England, Italy, Mexico, Peru, Uruguay, the USSR and West Germany. The four quarter final matches produced 17 goals.

The tie of the round was the meeting in Leon between England and West Germany, a repeat of the 1966 Final.

Gordon Banks had to miss this match with a stomach upset, and Peter Bonetti of Chelsea took his place in goal. England took a two-goal lead through Alan Mullery and Martin Peters, then Franz Beckenbauer pulled one back for the Germans. The game looked like England's, and manager Alf Ramsey took the historic decision to take off Peters and Bobby Charlton and replace them with Francis Lee and Norman Hunter. This changed the balance of the side and the course of the match - shortly after the twin substitution, Uwe Seeler equalised for West Germany. In extra time, Geoff Hurst had an effort disallowed before Gerd Muller scored the winner.

In the semi-finals, Italy beat West Germany 4-3 after extra time and Brazil beat Uruguay 3-1.

The 1970 World Cup Final between Brazil and Italy was held in the Aztec Stadium, Mexico City on June 21 before a crowd of 107,000.

BRAZIL: Felix, Carlos Alberto, Brito, Piazza, Everaldo, Clodoaldo, Gerson, Jairzinho, Tostao, Pele, Rivelino
ITALY: Albertosi, Burgnich, Facchetti, Cera, Rosato, Bertini (sub: Juliano), Riva, Domenghini, Mazzola, De Sisti, Boninsegna (sub: Rivera)

In the first half, Pele headed Brazil into an early lead, but a defensive disaster allowed Boninsegna to equalise. In the second half Brazil took control and showed themselves to be the outstanding team of the tournament. They scored again through Gerson, Jairzinho and captain Carlos Alberto.

This was Brazil's third World Cup triumph and they thus kept the Jules Rimet Trophy.

The leading scorer in the 1970 World Cup finals was Gerd Muller of West Germany, with 10 goals in the tournament. Brazil's Jairzinho was second with seven and the veteran Peruvian Teofilo Cubillas third, with five goals.

Jairzinho also became the only player in the 20th century to score in every round of the World Cup finals.

THE SEVENTIES

Facts

In 1971, Arsenal became only the
second club this century - after
fierce local rivals Tottenham
Hotspur - to win the League
and FA Cup double.

Arsenal's manager was Bertie Mee,
their captain Frank McLintock.

**Runners-up were Leeds
United - their 64 points in
the season was the
highest number of
points that had ever failed to
secure the Championship.**

Fifth-placed Liverpool
conceded only 24 goals in the 1970-71 season - an all-time low.

**The First Division's leading scorer was Tony Brown, with 28 goals
for 17th-placed West Bromwich Albion.**

In the FA Cup Final, Arsenal beat Liverpool 2-1 after extra time. Liverpool
went ahead with a goal from Steve Heighway, and then Eddie Kelly became
the first substitute ever to score in an FA Cup Final. The winner came eight
minutes from time - scorer Charlie George.

**Among the giant-killers in this season's FA Cup were Barnet -
then a non-League club - who beat Fourth Division Newport
County 6-1.**

Tottenham Hotspur won the League Cup. They beat Aston Villa 2-0 in the Final, both their goals being scored by Martin Chivers, their record signing from Southampton in 1968.

The season was a disaster for the 'B's of Lancashire - Burnley and Blackpool were relegated from the First Division, Blackpool after only a year back in it; Blackburn Rovers and Bolton Wanderers - founder members of the League - were relegated to the Third Division for the first time in their histories.

North of the border, Celtic did the League and FA Cup double for the third time in five seasons. Their - and Scotland's - leading scorer was Harry Hood, with 22 goals in the season.

Rangers prevented Celtic from doing the treble by beating them 1-0 in the Final of the Scottish League Cup. It was five years since Rangers had won a trophy - their last success had been in the 1966 FA Cup Final. This was the longest barren period in their history.

This season, the Scottish League introduced goal difference instead of goal average as a means of separating teams level on points.

Ajax of Amsterdam won the European Cup for the first time, beating Greek League Champions Panathinaikos 2-0 in the Final at Wembley.

Chelsea won the Cup Winners' Cup, beating Real Madrid 2-1 after extra time in the Final replay after the first match had been drawn 1-1. Peter Osgood scored in both games; Chelsea's other goal came from John Dempsey. Both games were played in Athens.

In the semi-final of the Cup Winners' Cup, Chelsea had eliminated the holders, Manchester City, 1-0 on aggregate.

The Seventies

Leeds United finally won a trophy - the Inter-Cities Fairs Cup for the second time. They drew with Juventus 3-3 in the Final, but took the Cup on away goals after their 2-2 draw in the first leg in Turin.

This was the last season of the Inter-Cities Fairs Cup. The following year it was replaced by the UEFA Cup. It was also the fourth year running that it had been won by an English club.

The 1972 English First Division Championship was won by Derby County, the first League title in their history.

Derby had finished the 1966-67 season in 17th place in Division Two. But then Brian Clough and Peter Taylor took over the management of the club and the upturn in their fortunes began. They won the Second Division Championship in 1969, then came fourth in the First Division in 1970 and ninth in 1971.

The First Division's leading scorer was Francis Lee of Manchester City. Of his 33 League goals, 13 were penalties - an all-time record. Many of these spot kicks were the result of fouls on the player himself - this gave rise to his Oriental-sounding nickname Lee Won Pen.

154

Leeds United won the 100th FA Cup, beating the holders, Arsenal, 1-0 in the Final with a goal from Allan Clarke.

Arsenal reached Wembley the hard way - for the second season running, they did not have a single home draw in the competition.

FA Cup giantkillers of the season were Hereford United - then still a non-League club - who drew 2-2 with First Division Newcastle United at St James' Park and then beat them 2-1 at Edgar Street with goals from Ronnie Radford and Ricky George.

Leeds were again runners-up in the First Division. This was despite having been ordered to play their first four home matches away from Elland Road - a punishment for a pitch invasion in April.

This was the year in which Leeds almost bought Asa Hartford from West Bromwich Albion, but pulled out of the deal after a medical examination revealed that the player had a hole in his heart. Despite this condition, Hartford went on to play with great distinction for several clubs, including Manchester City - where he won two League Cup winner's medals - and 50 times for Scotland.

Stoke City won the League Cup - the first trophy in their history - beating Chelsea 2-1 in the Final at Wembley. Their goals were scored by Terry Conroy and veteran George Eastham, aged 35. Chelsea's goal was scored by Peter Osgood.

The great match of the season's League Cup was Stoke's epic semi-final against West Ham United. Stoke lost the first leg 2-1 but levelled the tie at Upton Park. Then, with three minutes of extra time remaining, Stoke's England keeper Gordon Banks saved a penalty from Geoff Hurst.

The first West Ham v Stoke play-off, at Hillsborough, ended goalless, so a second replay was held at Old Trafford. West Ham's keeper Bobby Ferguson was hurt in this match and had to leave the field. His place in goal was taken by captain Bobby Moore, who saved a penalty, but Mike Bernard scored from the rebound.

West Ham plugged on with 10 men - they expected Ferguson to return - and took the lead with goals by Billy Bonds and Trevor Brooking. But Stoke equalised through Peter Dobing and scored the winner shortly after half time through Terry Conroy.

In Scotland, Celtic again did the double. They won the League Championship by 10 points from second-placed Aberdeen and beat Hibernian 6-1 in the Final of the FA Cup.

Surprisingly, however, Celtic were beaten 4-1 in the League Cup Final by unfancied Partick Thistle. This was only Thistle's second trophy - their previous triumph had been in the 1921 FA Cup.

Partick Thistle's goals came in the first 37 minutes through Alex Rae, Bobby Lawrie, Denis McQuade and Jimmy Bone. Celtic's reply was scored by Kenny Dalglish.

Ajax Amsterdam retained the European Cup, beating Inter Milan 2-0 in the Final in Rotterdam. Star of the match was European Footballer of the Year Johan Cruyff.

Rangers won the Cup Winners' Cup, for which they had only qualified as losing FA Cup finalists because Celtic did the double and went into the European Cup. They beat Moscow Dynamo 3-2 in the Final in Barcelona, with one goal from Colin Stein and two from Willie Johnston.

Rangers never defended their trophy. The match was marred by pitch invasions by their fans, and as a result the club was banned from European competition for a year.

The first UEFA Cup Final was an all-England affair, Tottenham Hotspur beating Wolverhampton Wanderers 3-2 on aggregate. They won the first leg at Molineux 2-1, with two goals by Martin Chivers. Wolves' scorer was Jim McCalliog. At White Hart Lane, Alan Mullery increased the London club's lead, but David Wagstaffe equalised for Wolves. Spurs thus became the first English club to win two different European trophies - they had lifted the Cup Winners' Cup in 1963.

In the European Championship, England were eliminated by West Germany after losing 3-1 at Wembley. The German star was Gunter Netzer, who scored from a penalty and set up two goals for Gerd Muller. In the second leg, although England brought in Norman Hunter to neutralise Netzer, they could only draw 0-0 and were knocked out.

The semi-finals and Final of the 1972 European Championship were held in Belgium. West Germany beat the hosts 2-1, while in the other match the USSR beat Hungary 1-0.

The Final was held in Brussels on June 18, 1972. West Germany beat the USSR 3-0 with another two goals from Muller and one from Wimmer.

In 1973, Liverpool won the League Championship for a record eighth time.

The First Division's leading scorer was Bryan 'Pop' Robson, with 28 goals for West Ham United.

The Champions of all four Divisions of the Football League came from Lancashire - Liverpool won the First Division, Burnley the Second, Bolton Wanderers the Third and Southport the Fourth.

Sunderland became the first Second Division side to win the FA Cup since West Bromwich Albion in 1931 when they beat Leeds United 1-0 in the Final at Wembley with a goal from Ian Porterfield. Thereafter, Jim Montgomery held Leeds at bay almost singlehandedly with a magnificent display in goal.

Tottenham Hotspur won the League Cup, beating Norwich City 1-0 in the Final. Spurs' winner was scored by Ralph Coates.

In May 1973, Derby County bought Leicester City full back David Nish for £225,000, a British record transfer fee.

Huddersfield Town - three times League Champions - were relegated to the Third Division for the first time in their history.

In Scotland, Celtic won the League Championship and finished runners-up in both the Cups.

Rangers took the Scottish FA Cup in their centenary year, beating Celtic 3-2 in the Final with goals from Parlane, Conn and Forsyth. Celtic opened the scoring through Dalglish, and later brought the game back to 2-2 with a penalty scored by Scottish Footballer of the Year George Connelly.

Hibernian won the Scottish League Cup, beating Celtic 2-1 in the Final.

Ajax of Amsterdam won the European Cup for the third year in succession, beating Juventus 1-0 in the Final in Belgrade.

AC Milan won the Cup Winners' Cup, beating Leeds United 1-0 in the Final in Salonika. Yet again, Leeds finished empty-handed a season that had promised so much - they had nearly won the League, but finished third, lost in the FA Cup Final to unfancied opposition, and now this defeat by an Italian team they outplayed for much of the match.

Liverpool won the 1973 UEFA Cup, beating Borussia Moenchengladbach 3-2 on aggregate in the Final.

Leeds United won the League Championship in 1974 for the second time in their history. At the start of the season, they went 23 matches without defeat - a record.

Promotion and relegation changed from two- to three-up and down between the First and Second and the Second and Third Divisions. The first club to be relegated from the First Division after finishing 20th out of 22 was Southampton.

The First Division's leading scorer was Mike Channon, with 21 goals for relegated Southampton.

Manchester United finished 21st (next to last) and were relegated - they had been in the First Division since 1938. Their final match was at home to local rivals Manchester City - they lost 1-0, and the goal was scored by ex-United hero Denis Law. Shortly afterwards, a massive pitch invasion led the referee to abandon the match on the advice of police, but the result stood.

In his first season as a manager, England World Cup hero Jack Charlton guided Middlesbrough to the Second Division Championship, thus getting them back into the top flight for the first time since 1954.

On September 22, 1973, three Notts County players missed the same penalty in their Second Division match against Portsmouth at Fratton Park.

The Eagles of Crystal Palace went into a free fall, as they were relegated from the First to the Third Division of the League in successive seasons.

Fourth Division Exeter City unilaterally cancelled their League match against Scunthorpe United because they had nine players unfit. In doing this, they risked expulsion from the League, but escaped with a fine of £5000 and two points (the League awarded the game to Scunthorpe).

League runners-up Liverpool won the FA Cup, beating Newcastle United 3-0 in the Final. Their goals were scored by Kevin Keegan (2) and Steve Heighway.

At 11 o'clock on the morning of January 6, 1974, professional football was played on Sunday in England for the first time - Cambridge United drew 2-2 with Oldham Athletic in the third round of the FA Cup.

Wolverhampton Wanderers won the League Cup Final, beating Manchester City 2-1 in the Final.

Plymouth Argyle of the Third Division reached the League Cup semi-finals. En route, they beat three First Division clubs away - Burnley, Queen's Park Rangers and Birmingham City - before losing 3-1 on aggregate to Manchester City, the eventual runners-up.

Celtic won the Scottish Championship for the ninth year in a row. They also did the double, beating Dundee United 3-0 in the Final of the Scottish FA Cup.

Celtic's - and the Scottish First Division's - leading scorer was Dixie Deans, with 24 goals.

Dundee won the Scottish League Cup was won by Dundee, who beat Celtic 1-0 in the Final.

In the first European Cup Final to require a replay, Bayern Munich eventually beat Atletico Madrid 4-1 after the first match had been drawn 1-1. Both games were played in Brussels.

Feyenoord of Rotterdam made it a double Dutch Cup celebration when they beat Tottenham Hotspur 4-2 on aggregate in the Final of the UEFA Cup. The second leg was marred by Spurs fans who rioted in the stadium and had to be dispersed by Dutch police.

FC Magdeburg of East Germany won the Cup Winners' Cup, beating AC Milan 2-0 in the Final in Rotterdam.

On September 26, 1973, Trevor Hockey of Aston Villa became the first Welsh player to be sent off in an international during his country's 3-0 defeat by Poland in Katowice in the World Cup qualifying match.

England were knocked out of the World Cup when they finished behind Poland in their qualifying group. The killer blow came when the Poles came to Wembley and went ahead through Domarski who shot under Peter Shilton's body after 58 minutes. The rest of the match was sustained England pressure, and although they salvaged a draw with a penalty from Allan Clarke, the home team were denied the win they needed by Polish keeper Jan Tomaszewski, memorably - but inaccurately - described by Brian Clough on television as 'a clown'.

In the aftermath of England's failure to reach the World Cup finals, the FA sacked Sir Alf Ramsey. Of their 113 matches under Ramsey, England had won 69 and drawn 27 and one of these victories had been their greatest triumph - the 1966 World Cup Final. There was widespread distaste that, given his distinguished record, Sir Alf had not been given the opportunity to resign.

Sir Alf Ramsey was replaced by Joe Mercer, who took over as England caretaker-manager while a long-term successor was sought.

Three days before the opening ceremony of the 1974 World Cup finals, Brazilian Joao Havelange replaced Sir Stanley Rous as President of FIFA.

The 1974 World Cup finals were held in West Germany. The 16 qualifying nations were Argentina, Australia, Brazil, Bulgaria, Chile, East Germany, Haiti, Holland, Italy, Poland, Scotland, Sweden, Uruguay, West Germany, Yugoslavia and Zaire.

In a departure from the practice in previous tournaments, goal difference was brought in for the first time to separate teams equal on points in the qualifying groups.

In another change to previous formats, the top two teams in each of the four qualifying groups were to progress into two more groups of four - the winners of these two groups would contest the Final, which would thus become the only true knockout match in the entire tournament.

Scotland went out in the group stage, but only because they scored one goal fewer than Brazil against Zaire. Quite how close they came to reaching the second stage may be seen from the Group Two Final Table:

	P	W	D	L	F	A	Pts
Yugoslavia	3	1	2	0	10	1	4
Brazil	3	1	2	0	3	0	4
Scotland	3	1	2	0	3	1	4
Zaire	3	0	0	3	0	14	0

The shock of round one was the 1-0 defeat of hosts and favourites West Germany by their neighbours East Germany.

Poland - who had been regarded as no-hopers, even after they had qualified at England's expense - won Group Four at a canter, with maximum points against Argentina, Italy and Haiti. They eventually finished third in the tournament and had the two leading scorers - Grzegorz Lato with seven goals and Andrzej Szarmach with five.

In the second round, Group A contained Argentina, Brazil, East Germany and Holland; in Group B were Poland, Sweden, West Germany and Yugoslavia.

The winners of these groups were West Germany and Holland, each with hundred per cent records.

The 1974 World Cup Final was played at the Olympic Stadium, Munich, on July 7, 1974, before a crowd of 77,833.

West Germany: Maier, Vogts, Schwarzenbeck, Beckenbauer, Breitner, Hoeness, Bonhof, Overath, Grabowski, Muller, Holzenbein
Holland: Jongbloed, Suurbier, Rijsbergen (sub: De Jong), Haan, Krol, Jansen, Neeskens, Van Hanegem, Rep, Cruyff, Rensenbrink (sub: R. Van Der Kerkhof)

Holland scored before a German had touched the ball when Uli Hoeness fouled Johann Cruyff inside the penalty area and Johan Neeskens scored from the spot.

This was the first penalty in a World Cup Final. The referee who awarded it was Englishman Jack Taylor.

The second penalty in a World Cup Final came less than 25 minutes later. This time, it went to West Germany after Holzenbein had been fouled in the box. Paul Breitner took the spot kick and made the score 1-1.

Two minutes before half-time, Bonhof fed Gerd Muller in the area - he swivelled and scored what turned out to be the World Cup-winning goal for West Germany.

The 1974-75 season began with the unprecedented spectacle of a double sending-off in the Charity Shield match between last year's Champions Leeds United and the FA Cup winners Liverpool. The two to get their marching orders for fighting were no less than the international stars Billy Bremner and Kevin Keegan - the first Britons ever to be sent off at Wembley. They were later fined £500 each and banned for what turned out to be 11 matches.

Derby County won the League Championship for the second time in four years, this time under the management of Dave Mackay.

Brian Clough and Peter Taylor had quit Derby after the former had refused to accept an ultimatum from the club that he stop writing for the newspapers and appearing on television. Derby chairman Sam Longston was particularly concerned about Clough's accusation that some of his own players were giving less than one hundred per cent.

The First Division's leading scorer in 1974-75 was Malcolm Macdonald, with 21 goals for Newcastle United.

Malcolm Macdonald also became the only player to score five goals in a Wembley international when England beat Cyprus 5-0 in the European Championships.

Manchester United came straight back up, winning the Second Division Championship at their first attempt.

West Ham United won the FA Cup in 1975, beating Fulham 2-0 in the Final. Both their Wembley goals were scored by Alan Taylor.

Taylor - purchased from Rochdale shortly before Christmas - had also scored two goals for West Ham in the sixth round versus Arsenal and in the semi-final replay versus Ipswich Town.

Playing for Fulham in that Final was West Ham's former captain and greatest legend - Bobby Moore.

The 1975 League Cup was won by Aston Villa, who beat Norwich City 1-0 in the Final. This was Norwich's second defeat at Wembley in this competition - they had been beaten by Spurs in the 1973 Final.

For Villa manager Ron Saunders, it was third time lucky - this was his third consecutive match in charge of a League Cup finalist, but on the two previous occasions he had seen his team lose - with Manchester City in 1974 and the year before with Norwich.

In Scotland, Celtic's great run of victories came to an end after nine League titles in a row - Rangers won their first title since 1964.

The joint leading scorers in the Scottish First Division were Andy Gray of Dundee United and Willie Pettigrew of Motherwell, each with 20 goals.

Celtic won the 1975 Scottish FA Cup, beating Airdrieonians 3-1 in the Final, which was European Cup-winning captain Billy McNeill's swansong for the club as a player.

The League Cup also went to Celtic, who beat Hibernian 6-3 in the Final.

Bayern Munich won the European Cup for the second year running, beating Leeds United 2-0 in the Final in Paris. The English Champions were incredibly unlucky in this match - they had two legitimate-looking penalty appeals against Beckenbauer turned down by French referee Kitabdjian, and a second-half goal by Peter Lorimer disallowed for offside. The Leeds fans rioted. There have since been strong and persistent rumours that the result was somehow fixed.

In an all-Eastern European Final, Dynamo Kiev of the USSR beat Ferencvaros of Hungary 2-0 to win the Cup Winners' Cup.

Borussia Moenchengladbach (West Germany) won the UEFA Cup, beating Twente Enschede (Holland) 5-1 on aggregate in the Final.

On July 4, 1974, the FA announced the appointment of Leeds United boss Don Revie as Sir Alf Ramsey's permanent successor as England manager.

Revie was succeeded at Leeds by Brian Clough, the man who had taken Derby County to their first League title and then taken over at Brighton and Hove Albion. He lasted only 43 days in the post, unable to make an impact on the well-established cliques among the senior players in the Leeds dressing room.

During the 1974-75 season, three England international players went absent without leave - Kevin Keegan, Stan Bowles and Kevin Beattie.

After 15 years in charge at Anfield, Bill Shankly announced that he was stepping down as manager of Liverpool. Under him, Liverpool won the Second Division in 1962, the League Championship in 1964,1966 and 1973, the FA Cup in 1965 and 1974, and the UEFA Cup in 1973.

Bill Nicholson, for 38 years a Tottenham Hotspur employee and their manager since 1958, also announced his retirement. He gave as his reason the unreasonable demands and expectations of modern players. Under Nicholson, Spurs had won the double in 1961, two more FA Cups in 1962 and 1967, the Cup Winners' Cup in 1963 and the UEFA Cup in 1972.

In 1975-76, Liverpool won the League Championship for a record ninth time and the first time under Bob Paisley in his first season as manager in succession to Bill Shankly. They pipped Queen's Park Rangers to the title by a single point.

The First Division's leading scorer in 1975-76 was Ted MacDougall, with 23 goals for 16th-placed Norwich City.

Second Division Southampton won the 1976 FA Cup - the first major honour in their history - beating the favourites Manchester United 1-0 in the Final. The winning goal was scored by Bobby Stokes.

Manchester City won the League Cup for the second time, beating Newcastle United 2-1 in the Final. Peter Barnes and Denis Tueart scored for the winners; Alan Gowling replied for the Magpies.

In Scotland, the League was reorganised yet again. The two old Divisions - the First of 18 clubs the Second of 20 - were changed into a Premier League of 10 clubs and a First and Second Division, each of 14 clubs.

Rangers did the treble, winning the League, the Cup and the League Cup. They retained the Championship and thus became the first winners of the new Premier League. They beat Heart of Midlothian 3-1 in the FA Cup Final and Celtic 1-0 in the League Cup Final.

The leading scorer in the Scottish Premier Division was Kenny Dalglish, with 24 goals for Celtic.

Bayern Munich won the European Cup for the third time running, beating St Etienne of France 1-0 in the Final.

Anderlecht of Belgium won the Cup Winners' Cup, beating West Ham United 4-2 in the Final in Brussels.

West Ham United came close to repeating their 1965 Cup Winners' Cup triumph. They went ahead with a goal from Pat Holland and were on top until Frank Lampard injured himself while trying to pass back to keeper Mervyn Day - the ball fell short and Dutch international Robbie Rensenbrink scored easily. In the second half, Anderlecht took the lead with a goal from François Van Der Elst, but West Ham got back on level terms with a goal from 'Pop' Robson. But after that, Anderlecht took charge - Holland brought down Rensenbrink, who scored from the penalty spot, and then Van der Elst broke through on his own, rounded the West Ham right back and keeper and scored a brilliant individual clinching goal.

League Champions Liverpool did a unique double by also winning the UEFA Cup, beating FC Bruges of Belgium 4-3 on aggregate in the Final. This was Liverpool's second UEFA Cup in four years.

The semi-finals and Final of the 1976 European Championship were held in Yugoslavia. In the semi-finals, Czechoslovakia beat Holland 3-1 and West Germany beat Yugoslavia 4-2.

The Final between Czechoslovakia and West Germany, the holders and World Champions, was played in Belgrade on June 20, 1976, in front of 45,000 spectators. The Czechs went two up with goals from Svehlik and Dobias; the Germans pulled one back through Dieter Muller and equalised through Holzenbein in the dying seconds of normal time. The score remained unchanged at the end of extra time and the Championship had to be decided on a penalty shoot-out, which the Czechs won 5-3.

At the start of the 1976-77 season, the English Football League abolished goal average - from now on, teams equal on points would be separated by goal difference (the number of goals they had conceded subtracted from the number of goals they had scored).

1976-77 was the first League season in which yellow and red cards replaced (respectively) the notebook and the finger pointed towards the tunnel.

Liverpool retained the League Championship, a point ahead of Manchester City in second place.

Joint leading scorers with 25 in the First Division were Malcolm Macdonald, formerly of Newcastle United but now of eighth-placed Arsenal, and Andy Gray of fourth-placed Aston Villa.

Manchester United won the FA Cup, beating Liverpool 2-1 in the Final. Stuart Pearson scored the first, Jimmy Case equalised for Liverpool and then Jimmy Greenhoff scored the winner with a fluke as he tried to get out of the way of a shot from Lou Macari.

Aston Villa won the League Cup after a marathon Final against Everton. The first match finished 0-0; the replay was 1-1 after extra time. The second replay went to extra time before Villa clinched it 3-2, with two goals from Brian Little and another by Chris Nicholl. Everton's replies came from Bob Latchford and Mick Lyons.

Terry Paine of Southampton retired at the end of the season after 824 League appearances - a record.

Bobby Moore - now of Fulham, but famously of West Ham and England - retired at the end of his 1000th first class match on May 14 at Blackburn.

After finishing bottom of the Fourth Division for the second year running - and next to bottom in both previous seasons - Workington failed to win re-election. Their place in the Football League was taken by Wimbledon.

In Scotland, Celtic did the double. They won the Premier Division by nine points from second-placed Rangers and beat the same club 1-0 in the Final of the FA Cup.

Celtic's dreams of another treble were shattered by a 2-1 defeat by Aberdeen in the Final of the League Cup.

Liverpool more than made up for their FA Cup Final disappointment by beating Borussia Moenchengladbach 3-1 in the European Cup Final in Rome. Their goals were scored by Terry McDermott, Tommy Smith and Phil Neal (penalty). The German team's replay was scored by Danish international Allan Simonsen.

SV Hamburg won the Cup Winners' Cup, beating the holders Anderlecht 2-0 in the Final in Amsterdam.

Hamburg captured another prize at the end of the season - they bought Kevin Keegan from Liverpool for £500,000.

Juventus won the UEFA Cup on away goals after drawing 2-2 on aggregate in the Final with Athletic Bilbao.

Scotland won the Home International Championship and Wales won at Wembley for the first time in their history.

After three years in which the national team won only 14 times in 29 internationals, Don Revie resigned as England manager on July 12, 1977, and took a £60,000-a-year job as coach to the United Arab Emirates.

In July 1977, former West Ham manager Ron Greenwood took over from Revie as England manager. The appointment was temporary at first, but was soon extended to the end of the 1980 European Championship.

In his first match in charge - a 0-0 draw against Switzerland at Wembley on September 7 - Greenwood picked six Liverpool players plus a seventh - Kevin Keegan - who had been at the club until the end of last season. This was the highest number of players from a single club to represent England since seven Arsenal players took the field against Italy on November 14, 1934 - the notorious match that became known as The Battle of Highbury.

Shortly after selling Kevin Keegan to Hamburg, on August 10, 1977, Liverpool spent £400,000 on a replacement - 27-year-old Kenny Dalglish of Celtic.

Tommy Docherty was sacked as manager of Manchester United only six weeks after leading them to victory in the FA Cup Final because of tabloid revelations about his love affair with the wife of Laurie Brown, the Old Trafford club's physiotherapist .

Scotland qualified for the World Cup Finals in Argentina with a 2-0 victory over Wales in a play-off at neutral Anfield. The first goal was scored by Don Masson from a penalty which television replays showed should not have been awarded - the handler was not a Welshman but Scotland's Joe Jordan. The clincher was scored after 87 minutes by Kenny Dalglish with a header.

Liverpool were denied a third consecutive League title by Nottingham Forest, who won the Championship in their first season back in the First Division.

Among Forest's stars were goalkeeper Peter Shilton - the club's record £250,000 buy from Stoke City - and defender Kenny Burns, a player with a reputation as a wild man whom manager Brian Clough bought from Birmingham City for £150,000 and promptly made club captain. At the end of the season, Shilton was voted the PFA Player of the year; Burns won the Football Writers' award.

Having won the League with Derby County in 1972, Brian Clough now became only the second manager to lead two different clubs to the English Championship - the other was Herbert Chapman, who won it with Huddersfield Town and Arsenal in the 1930s.

Leading scorer in the First Division was Bob Latchford, with 30 goals for third-placed Everton.

On February 9, 1978, Manchester United bought Scottish international defender Gordon McQueen from Leeds United for a British record fee of £495,000.

Nottingham Forest did the so-called 'New Double' by winning the League Cup as well as the League. They drew 0-0 with Liverpool after extra time in the Wembley Final and then scraped home 1-0 in the replay at Old Trafford with a penalty by John Robertson.

In both the Final matches, Forest's goalkeeper was Chris Woods, who played because first choice Peter Shilton was Cup-tied.

Ipswich Town won the 1978 FA Cup, beating Arsenal 1-0 in the Final with a goal by Roger Osborne.

In Scotland, Rangers did the treble for the second time in three seasons. They won the League by two points from runners-up Aberdeen, beat them again in the FA Cup Final, by two goals to one, and beat Celtic 2-1 after extra time in the League Cup Final.

**Rangers' - and the Scottish First Division's - leading scorer was
Derek Johnstone, with 25 goals.**

Liverpool retained the European Cup, beating FC Bruges in the Final at
Wembley. The only goal of the game was scored in the 66th minute by
Kenny Dalglish.

**Anderlecht made it two Cup Winners' Cups in three years,
beating Austria/WAC 4-0 in the Final in Paris.**

PSV Eindhoven of Holland won the UEFA Cup, beating Bastia of France 3-0
on aggregate in the Final.

**The 1978 World Cup finals were held in Argentina. The 16
qualifying nations were Argentina, Austria, Brazil, France, Holland,
Hungary, Iran, Italy, Mexico, Peru, Poland, Scotland, Spain,
Sweden, Tunisia and West Germany.**

Scotland - Britain's only representatives in Argentina - had been enormously
hyped in the build-up to the finals, especially by their manager, Ally MacLeod.
This made their performance all the more of a let-down - they lost their
opening group match 3-1 to Peru and then almost guaranteed elimination by
managing only a 1-1 draw with widely unfancied Iran. In between these
matches, Willie Johnston failed a drugs test and was sent home in disgrace.

The Scots almost retrieved the situation with a 3-1 victory in their final group match against Holland. This was a magnificent performance, which owed much to Graeme Souness and Archie Gemmill, but it was too little, too late.

The eight nations who went through to the second round of the finals were Argentina, Austria, Brazil, Holland, Italy, Peru, Poland and West Germany.

Holland won Group A, beating Austria and Italy and drawing with West Germany, the holders.

Argentina won Group B, with victories over Poland and Peru and a draw with Brazil.

The 1978 World Cup Final was held in the River Plate Stadium, Buenos Aires on June 25, 1978 in front of a crowd of 77,260.

ARGENTINA: Fillol, Olguin, Galvan, Passarella, Tarantini, Ardiles (sub: Larrosa), Gallego, Kempes, Bertoni, Luque, Ortiz (sub: Houseman)
HOLLAND: Jongbloed, Poortvliet, Krol, Brandts, Jansen (sub: Suurbier), Neeskens, Haan, W. Van Der Kerkhof, R. Van Der Kerkhof, Rep (Sub: Nanninga), Rensenbrink

Mario Kempes, the tournament's leading scorer, put Argentina ahead after 38 minutes, but Holland equalised after 82 minutes through a header from Dirk Manninga, who had come on as substitute for Johnny Rep. Argentina pulled away in extra time, with another goal from Kempes and a clincher from Ricardo Bertoni after 115 minutes.

Just over a fortnight after winning the 1978 World Cup, two of Argentina's squad were signed by Tottenham Hotspur. Osvaldo Ardiles and Riccardo Villa came from Huracan and Racing Club respectively for a combined total of £750,000. The deal was brokered on Spurs' behalf by Sheffield United manager Harry Haslam.

Liverpool regained the League Championship, eight points ahead of last year's title-winners Nottingham Forest in second place. Their points total - 68- was a new record for the 22-club First Division under two points for a win. They also conceded only 16 goals in the season - an all-time low.

When Forest lost 2-0 at Liverpool on December 9, 1978, it was their first League defeat in 42 matches over one year and 13 days - the longest unbeaten run in the history of the Football League.

The First Division's leading scorer in 1978-79 was Frank Worthington of 17th-placed Bolton Wanderers.

Nottingham Forest had the consolation of retaining the League Cup, beating Southampton 3-2 in the 1979 Final. Forest's Wembley goals came from Garry Birtles (2) and Tony Woodcock; Southampton replied through David Peach and Nick Holmes.

Arsenal won the 1979 FA Cup, beating Manchester United 3-2 in one of the most exciting Finals for years. They went ahead in the first half with a goal by Brian Talbot, but then United scored twice in two minutes through Gordon McQueen and Sammy McIlroy. With a minute to go, Frank Stapleton levelled the scores again. Then, just as the crowd was preparing for extra time, Liam Brady broke down the left for Arsenal, then passed to Graham Rix who centred for Alan Sunderland to score the winner.

In Scotland, Celtic won the League Championship, finishing three points ahead of Rangers in second place.

Rangers did a Cup double. They won the Scottish FA Cup - beating Hibernian 3-2 in a second Final replay after the first two matches had ended goalless - and the League Cup with a 2-1 victory in the Final over Aberdeen.

Leading scorer in the Scottish Premier Division was Andy Ritchie, with 22 goals for seventh-placed Morton.

A new British transfer record was set in February 1979 - Trevor Francis became the first million-pound player when he moved from Birmingham City to Nottingham Forest.

The European Cup remained in England but moved from Liverpool to Nottingham. Forest beat FC Malmo in the Final in Munich. The only goal of the game was scored by million-pound man Trevor Francis.

European Cup holders Liverpool were knocked out in the second round of the 1978-79 competition by Nottingham Forest, the current English Champions and eventual winners of the Cup. Barcelona won the Cup Winners' Cup, beating Fortuna Dusseldorf 4-3 after extra time in the Final.

Borussia Moenchengladbach won the UEFA Cup, beating Red Star Belgrade 2-1 on aggregate in the Final.

On November 29, 1978, Viv Anderson of Nottingham Forest became the first black man to play for England in their 1-0 victory over Czechoslovakia in a friendly at Wembley.

Don Revie was banned for 10 years by the FA for walking out of his job as England manager in July 1977 to coach the United Arab Emirates. However, this ruling was later overturned by the High Court, which suggested that the football authorities might have been biased against their former employee.

In 1979-80, Liverpool won the League Championship for the second year running. This was their 12th title - a record.

The First Division's leading scorer was Phil Boyer, with 23 goals for eighth-placed Southampton.

West Ham United - currently a Second Division side - won the FA Cup for the third time in their history. Runners-up Arsenal were appearing in their third consecutive Final. The only goal at Wembley came from a first-half header by Trevor Brooking.

Wolverhampton Wanderers won the League Cup. They beat Nottingham Forest 1-0 in the Final with a goal from record signing Andy Gray after Forest defender David Needham collided with Peter Shilton after failing to hear the keeper's call.

Nottingham Forest retained the European Cup. In the Final in Madrid they won 1-0 against an SV Hamburg side that included Kevin Keegan. The winning goal was scored by John Robertson.

Valencia won the Cup Winners' Cup, beating Arsenal 5-4 on penalties after the Final had ended 0-0 after extra time. This was the first major Final to be decided by this method.

Eintracht Frankfurt won the UEFA Cup, beating the holders, Borussia Moenchengladbach in the Final on away goals after the two legs had finished 3-3 on aggregate.

In September 1979, the British transfer record was smashed twice in quick succession - first when Malcolm Allison of Manchester City signed Steve Daley of Wolverhampton Wanderers for £1,437,500, and again shortly afterwards when Wolves spent £1,469,000 on Aston Villa striker Andy Gray.

In February 1980, it was announced that next season European Footballer of the Year Kevin Keegan would be playing for Southampton after three years at Hamburg. The £400,000 transfer fee would almost certainly have been immensely higher had there not been an EEC-imposed limit of £500,000 on international transfers between clubs in different member states.

In Scotland, there was an unfamiliar name on the honours board as Aberdeen won the League Championship for only the second time in their history (the previous occasion had been in 1955).

The leading scorer in the Scottish Premier Division was Doug Somner, with 25 goals for third-placed St Mirren.

Celtic won the 1980 FA Cup, beating Rangers 1-0 after extra time in the Final.

Dundee United won their first major honour when they beat Aberdeen 3-0 in the 1980 League Cup Final replay at Dens Park, Dundee. The first match at Hampden had ended in a 0-0 draw after extra time. The Terrors' goals were scored by Willie Pettigrew (2) and Paul Sturrock.

Northern Ireland won the Home International Championship outright for the first time since 1914. They beat Wales 1-0 in Wrexham, drew 1-1 with England at Wembley and won 1-0 against Scotland in Belfast.

The 1980 European Championship was held in Italy. The eight qualifying nations were Belgium, Czechoslovakia, England, Greece, Holland, Italy, Spain and West Germany.

West Germany won the European Championship for the third time running when they beat Belgium in the Final in Rome on June 22, 1980. Horst Hrubesch scored both their goals in a 2-1 victory in front of 47,864 spectators.

THE EIGHTIES

In 1980-81, the FA stopped the red and yellow card system that had been introduced in 1976.

In 1981, Aston Villa won the League Championship for the seventh time in their history but the first time since 1910. They used only 14 players throughout the 42-match season.

With 20 goals apiece, joint leading scorers in the First Division were Steve Archibald of Tottenham Hotspur and Peter Withe of Aston Villa.

When they lost 2-1 at home to Leicester City on January 31, 1981, Liverpool suffered their first defeat at Anfield for three years and 10 days (85 matches in all competitions).

Tottenham Hotspur won the FA Cup for the sixth time in their history, beating Manchester City 3-2 in a replay after the first match - the 100th FA Cup Final - had finished 1-1 after extra time. In the first Final, City's Tommy Hutchison had scored for both sides - but not, as he has since been quick to point out to anyone who uses the wrong phrase, at both ends - his goal for City came in the first half and his own goal was scored in the second.

The hero of the replay - again held at Wembley - was Argentine Ricardo Villa, who had been substituted in the first match. He scored twice for Spurs, the second time after a fantastic dribble through a crowded City penalty area. Spurs' other goal was scored by Garth Crooks; City's goals came from Steve Mackenzie and a Kevin Reeves penalty.

Liverpool won the League Cup - the only domestic trophy that had previously eluded them - beating Second Division West Ham United 2-1 in a replay at Villa Park after the Wembley Final had ended 1-1 after extra time.

Liverpool regained the European Cup in 1981 after a two-year gap, beating Real Madrid in the Final in Paris with a goal by Alan Kennedy. This was Liverpool's third triumph in the competition and the fifth time running that the Cup had been won by an English club. One of the stars of the Real Madrid team was England international Laurie Cunningham.

Dynamo Tbilisi of the USSR won the Cup Winners' Cup, beating Carl Zeiss Jena of East Germany 2-1 in the Final in Dusseldorf.

In the second round of the Cup Winners' Cup, West Ham United had been forced to play the second leg of their match against Castilla of Spain behind closed doors after crowd trouble during the first match in Madrid.

Ipswich Town won the UEFA Cup, beating AZ 67 Alkmaar of Holland 5-4 on aggregate in the Final.

John Trollope of Swindon Town retired in November shortly after setting a new record for the number of League appearances for a single club - 770 since 1960. The previous record-holder had been Jimmy Dickinson, who played 764 games for Portsmouth between 1946 and 1965.

Celtic won the Scottish Premier Division - their 32nd League Championship. Their forward Frank McGarvey was the leading scorer, with 23 goals.

Rangers won the FA Cup, beating Dundee United 4-1 in a Final replay after the first match had ended goalless.

Dundee United retained the League Cup, beating Dundee 3-0 in the Final.

At the start of the 1981-82 season, the English Football League instituted three points for a win.

Second Division Queen's Park Rangers became the first English League club to install a plastic pitch. The material used was marketed under the name Omniturf.

The English transfer market boomed - enormous fees were paid for Justin Fashanu, who moved from Norwich City to Nottingham Forest for £1 million, Trevor Francis (£1.2 million from Nottingham Forest to Manchester City) and Frank Stapleton (Arsenal to Manchester United for £1.1 million). The biggest of the lot, however, was Bryan Robson, whose £1.7 million move from West Bromwich Albion to Manchester United was a new British record.

Liverpool won the League Championship for a record 13th time - their fifth title in seven seasons.

Liverpool also retained the League Cup (now renamed the Milk Cup), beating Tottenham Hotspur 3-1 after extra time in the 1982 Final. Their goals came from Ronnie Whelan (2) and Ian Rush; Spurs' reply came from Steve Archibald.

The First Division's leading scorer was Liverpool old boy Kevin Keegan, with 26 goals for his new club, Southampton.

Tottenham Hotspur retained the FA Cup, beating Second Division Queen's Park Rangers 1-0 in the Final replay after the first match had been drawn 1-1. Both Spurs' goals were scored by Glenn Hoddle, the second from the penalty spot.

Aston Villa won the 1982 European Cup, making it six in a row for English teams in this competition. They beat Bayern Munich in the Final in Rotterdam with a goal by Peter Withe.

Villa's victory came less than four months after Tony Barton had taken over as manager from Ron Saunders.

First-choice Villa keeper Jimmy Rimmer had to leave the field after only nine minutes of the Final because of a neck injury sustained during the pre-match warm-up. His place in goal was taken by Nigel Spink, playing in only his second game for the first team.

Barcelona won the Cup Winners' Cup in their own stadium, where they beat Standard Liege 2-1 in the Final.

IFK Gothenburg won the UEFA Cup, beating SV Hamburg 4-0 on aggregate in the Final.

In Scotland, Celtic won the League Championship. Their striker George McCluskey was the Premier Division's leading scorer, with 21 goals.

Aberdeen won the FA Cup, beating Rangers 4-1 in the Final after extra time.

Rangers won the League Cup, beating Dundee United 2-1 in the Final.

The 1982 World Cup finals were held in Spain. The tournament was now expanded to include 24 countries for the first time. The competing nations were Algeria, Argentina, Austria, Belgium, Brazil, Cameroon, Chile, Czechoslovakia, El Salvador, England, France, Honduras, Hungary, Italy, Kuwait, New Zealand, Northern Ireland, Peru, Poland, Scotland, Spain, the USSR, West Germany and Yugoslavia.

The surprise package in the first round of group matches was Cameroon, playing in their first finals. They were unbeaten against Italy, Peru and Poland and went out of the competition only because they had scored fewer goals than the Italians. Their stars were captain and keeper Thomas N'Kono and striker Roger Milla.

England had a hundred per cent record in the first round, beating France 3-1, Czechoslovakia 2-0 and Kuwait 1-0.

Scotland began the tournament by taking the lead against Brazil, but eventually lost 4-1. They then drew 2-2 with the USSR and, although they scored five goals against New Zealand, they carelessly conceded two - because of this they went out of the competition when a clean sheet would have seen them through to the second round.

Northern Ireland topped their group after drawing 0-0 with Yugoslavia and 1-1 with Honduras and then beating the hosts, Sapin, 1-0 with a goal by Gerry Armstrong.

The 12 countries that went forward to the second round of group matches were Argentina, Austria, Belgium, Brazil, England, France, Italy, Northern Ireland, Poland, Spain, the USSR and West Germany.

Most of the games between the three countries in each of the four groups were marred by defensive-mindedness. England drew their matches against Spain and West Germany and thus went out of the competition without having lost a match.

Northern Ireland drew with Austria but were soundly beaten 4-1 by France.

The four group winners - France, Italy, Poland and West Germany - went forward to the semi-finals, the first knockout matches of the 1982 tournament.

Italy beat Poland 2-0 and then France and West Germany drew 3-3 after extra time before the Germans won 5-4 on penalties.

The 1982 World Cup Final between Italy and West Germany was held in the Santiago Bernabeu Stadium, Madrid, on July 11 in front of 90,000 spectators.

ITALY: Zoff, Gentile, Collovati, Scirea, Cabrini, Conti, Oriali, Bergomi, Tardelli, Rossi, Graziani (subs: Altobelli, then Causio)
WEST GERMANY: Schumacher, Kaltz, K-H. Forster, Stielike, B. Forster, Briegel, Breitner, Dremmler (sub: Hrubesch), Littbarski, Fischer, Rummenigge (sub: Muller)

The main talking-point in the first half of the World Cup Final was a penalty miss by Cabrini. Italy eventually took the lead after 57 minutes with a goal by Paolo Rossi and then Marco Tardelli and Alessandro Altobelli made the Cup safe for Italy before West Germany's Paul Breitner became the first man to score in two World Cup Finals.

Paolo Rossi was the leading scorer in the 1982 World Cup finals, with six goals for Italy.

Shortly before the 1982 World Cup Final, the FA announced that the new England manager in succession to Ron Greenwood would be Bobby Robson of Ipswich Town.

In 1983, Liverpool won the Championship for the second year in succession and the sixth time in eight years. It was the 14th title in their history.

Runners-up were Watford, their highest ever League position in the year after they won promotion. Their leading scorer - and the First Division's - was Luther Blissett, with 27 goals.

Manchester United won the FA Cup in 1983 for the fifth time in their history, beating Brighton and Hove Albion 4-0 in the Final replay, with goals from Bryan Robson (2), Norman Whiteside and Arnold Muhren (penalty).

Facts

The first FA Cup Final had been drawn 2-2 - Frank Stapleton and Ray Wilkins scored for United, Gordon Smith and Gary Stevens for Brighton.

Brighton were also relegated in 1983, after three years in the First Division.

Liverpool retained the League (Milk) Cup, beating Manchester United 2-1 in the 1983 Final. United took the lead after 12 minutes with a goal by Norman Whiteside, but Liverpool fought back, drawing level with a goal by Alan Kennedy. Ronnie Whelan scored the winning goal in extra time.

On his 12th and final visit to Wembley, Bob Paisley became the first manager to lead his team up and collect a major trophy.

In Scotland, Dundee United won the League for the first time in their history under the management of Jim McLean.

Leading scorer was Charlie Nicholas, with 29 goals for second-placed Celtic.

Aberdeen became the first Scottish club this century other than Celtic and Rangers to retain the FA Cup, beating Rangers 1-0 after extra time in the Final. They then proceeded to do a Cup double, beating Real Madrid 2-1 in the Final of the Cup Winners' Cup in Gothenburg, Sweden.

Celtic won the League Cup, beating Rangers 2-1 in the Final.

SV Hamburg won the European Cup, beating Juventus 1-0 in the Final in Athens.

Anderlecht won the 1983 UEFA Cup, beating Benfica 2-1 on aggregate in the Final over two legs.

In 1983-84, for the first time in its history, the English First Division had a commercial sponsor - the Japanese-based camera-makers Canon.

Liverpool - now under the management of Joe Fagan - won the League Championship for the 15th time. This was one of three major trophies lifted by Liverpool this season. They also retained the Milk Cup, beating Everton 1-0 in the Final replay after the first match had been drawn 0-0. Then they won the European Cup for the fourth time, beating AS Roma 4-2 on penalties after the match had ended 1-1.

Liverpool's - and the First Division's, and Europe's leading scorer - was Ian Rush, with 32 goals.

Everton won the FA Cup, beating Watford 2-0 in the Final with goals by Graeme Sharp and Andy Gray.

The season's great giantkillers were both from the Third Division - Plymouth Argyle reached the semi-final of the FA Cup and Walsall reached the same stage of the Milk Cup.

In Scotland, Aberdeen did the double. They won the League Championship for the third time in their history - their previous victories had been in 1955 and 1980. They also became the first club other than Rangers to win the FA Cup three years running, beating Celtic 2-1 in the 1984 Final. Like their two previous Cup wins, this one was achieved after extra time.

Rangers won the League Cup, beating Celtic 3-2 after extra time in the Final.

Juventus won the 1984 Cup Winners' Cup Final, beating FC Porto 2-1 in the Final in Basle.

Tottenham Hotspur won the UEFA Cup 5-4 in a penalty shoot-out at White Hart Lane after each leg had been drawn 1-1.

Northern Ireland won the last Home International Championship on goal difference after all four countries finished with three points. The competition was not held again after England and Scotland withdrew because of fears for their safety in Belfast.

The finals of the 1984 European Championship were held in France. The eight qualifying nations were Belgium, Denmark, France, Portugal, Romania, Spain, West Germany and Yugoslavia.

France beat Portugal 3-2 in one semi-final; the other, between Denmark and Spain, finished 1-1 after extra time but Spain won the penalty shoot-out 5-4.

The European Championship Final was held at the Parc des Princes, Paris on June 27, 1984, in front of 80,000 spectators. France, the hosts, won the competition for the first time, beating Spain 2-0 with goals by Platini and Bellone.

The 1984-85 season was overshadowed by two great tragedies - the Bradford fire and the Heysel Stadium disaster.

On May 11, 1985, 56 people were burned to death, 70 more detained in hospital with severe burns, and a further 211 supporters and police injured when a timber stand caught fire at Bradford City's Valley Parade ground during an end-of-season match against Lincoln City. The game was fairly well attended, because Bradford had just ensured promotion from the old English Third Division, and many fans had come to celebrate.

The fire began amid rubbish which had accumulated beneath the stand over a long period and had never been swept up. Turnstiles had been locked to prevent latecomers getting in without paying. To make matters worse, there were no fire extinguishers in this part of the ground: they had been removed and stored in a room in the clubhouse because during previous games they been set off and used as missiles by unruly fans.

The Heysel Stadium disaster took place on May 29, 1985 just before the kick-off in the European Cup Final between Juventus and Liverpool in Brussels, Belgium. Thirty-nine people - most of them Italians - were killed and 454 others injured, many seriously, when groups of rival supporters charged each other through Block Z, which had been reserved for neutral spectators. Contributory factors included the easy availability of alcohol, poor segregation and inadequate safety barriers.

The League Championship moved across Stanley Park from Anfield to Goodison Park. It was the eighth title in Everton's history.

Everton also won the 1985 Cup Winners' Cup, beating Rapid Vienna 3-1 in the Final in Rotterdam.

With 24 goals apiece, the joint leading scorers in the First Division were Kerry Dixon of sixth-placed Chelsea and Gary Lineker of 15th-placed Leicester City.

Manchester United prevented a Goodison double by beating Everton 1-0 in the FA Cup Final. The winning goal was scored by Norman Whiteside.

Kevin Moran of Manchester United became the first player ever to be sent off in an FA Cup Final when he was dismissed by referee Peter Willis for a foul on Peter Reid.

Norwich City won the 1985 League Cup, beating Sunderland 1-0 in the Final. Both clubs were relegated from Division One at the end of the season.

Aberdeen retained the Scottish League Championship, finishing on 59 points, seven ahead of runners-up Celtic. Their leading scorer - and Scotland's - was Frank McDougall, with 24 goals.

Rangers won the 1985 League Cup - now renamed the Skol Cup - with a 1-0 Final victory over Dundee United.

Dundee United were again unlucky in the FA Cup, losing 2-1 in the Final to Celtic.

Real Madrid won the 1985 UEFA Cup, beating Videoton of Hungary 3-1 on aggregate in the Final.

Queen's Park Rangers - who qualified for the UEFA Cup by finishing fifth in 1984 - had to play their home matches in the competition at Highbury because UEFA refused to allow them to play on the synthetic pitch they had installed in 1981.

In the UEFA Cup second round, first leg, Queen's Park Rangers beat Partizan Belgrade 6-2 but lost the return 4-0 and went out of the competition.

In spite of the Heysel Stadium disaster, the European Cup Final went ahead as scheduled, kicking off 85 minutes late. Juventus won 1-0, the winning goal coming from a penalty by Michel Platini.

In the aftermath of Heysel, all English clubs were banned from European competitions. None was allowed back until 1990; Liverpool were readmitted in 1991. Joe Fagan stepped down and handed over to Kenny Dalglish, who became Liverpool's first player-manager.

In 1985-86, Liverpool won the double. Their League Championship was their eighth in 11 seasons and the 16th in their history. They finished two points ahead of last year's Champions, Everton, who came second.

Liverpool also beat Everton in the FA Cup Final. The score in the first ever Merseyside Cup Final was 3-1 - Liverpool's goals came from Ian Rush (2) and Craig Johnston.

Everton's goal in the 1986 FA Cup Final was scored by Footballer of the Year Gary Lineker. Lineker was also the First Division's leading scorer, with 30 goals.

A year after winning the Second Division Championship, Oxford United won the League (Milk) Cup, beating Queen's Park Rangers 3-0 in the Final with goals by Trevor Hebberd, Ray Houghton and Jeremy Charles.

On their way to the Third Division Championship, Reading created a new League record by winning their first 13 games of the season.

In Scotland, Celtic won the League Championship for the 34th time, finishing ahead of second-placed Heart of Midlothian on goal difference.

Scottish Premier Division 1985-86 Top of Table

	P	W	D	L	F	A	Pts
Celtic	36	20	10	6	67	38	50
Heart of Midlothian	36	20	10	6	59	33	50

Fifth-placed Rangers announced the appointment of Graeme Souness as player-manager in succession to Jock Wallace. The former Middlesbrough, Liverpool and Sampdoria midfielder had played 54 times for Scotland.

Aberdeen did a domestic double, winning both the FA Cup and the League Cup. They beat Heart of Midlothian 3-0 in the FA Cup Final, with two goals from John Hewitt and one from John Stark. In the League Cup Final, they beat Hibernian by the same score, two of their goals this time coming from Eric Black and another from John Stark.

Steua Bucharest of Romania won the European Cup, beating Barcelona 2-0 on penalties after the Final in Seville had finished 0-0 after extra time.

Facts

Dynamo Kiev won the Cup Winners' Cup, beating Atletico Madrid 3-0 in the Final in Lyon.

Real Madrid won the UEFA Cup, beating Cologne 5-3 on aggregate in the Final.

The 1986 World Cup was held in Mexico, which thus became the first country to stage the tournament twice. It had originally been awarded to Colombia, but it was subsequently decided that the country was too politically and socially unstable, and that the personal safety of those attending could not be guaranteed.

The 24 nations that reached this stage of the competition were Algeria, Argentina, Belgium, Brazil, Bulgaria, Canada, Denmark, England, France, Hungary, Iraq, Italy, Mexico, Morocco, Northern Ireland, Paraguay, Poland, Portugal, Scotland, South Korea, Spain, Uruguay, the USSR and West Germany.

England lost their opening match 1-0 to Portugal, then drew 0-0 with Morocco in a match in which Ray Wilkins was sent off for throwing the ball at the referee.

England came good in their final group match. Captain Bryan Robson's shoulder injury forced manager Bobby Robson to rejig his team's formation - Peter Beardsley replaced Mark Hateley up front; Gary Lineker responded by scoring all the goals in their 3-0 victory over Poland.

Scotland lost their first two matches - 1-0 to Denmark and 2-1 to West Germany. After less than a minute of their final game, Jose Batista of their opponents Uruguay was sent off. But the Scots could not capitalise on their numerical advantage - a 0-0 draw was not enough to keep them in the World Cup.

Northern Ireland found themselves in the what was probably the toughest group of the finals. They drew their opening game against Algeria but lost 2-1 to Spain and 3-0 to Brazil.

FIFA again altered the format of the World Cup finals. Although commencing the knockout stage in the second round was preferable to the stultifying groups of three there had been in Spain in 1982, the problem was how to reduce 24 finalists to 16. The solution - taking the top two in each group of four and adding the four best-place third teams - was unsatisfactory.

Belgium and Poland clearly deserved to go through to the next stage of the competition, finishing third in their groups with three points each. But although both Bulgaria and Portugal finished with two points and a goal difference of minus two, only Bulgaria went through. Uruguay took the 16th second round berth simply because they had finished third in their group - the fact that they had two points and a goal difference of minus five - inferior to Portugal's record - was discounted, and it was the Portuguese who went home.

In the second round of the1986 World Cup finals, England beat Paraguay 3-0 (two more for Lineker) and Argentina beat Uruguay 1-0. The two victorious nations then met each other in one of the greatest - and most controversial - matches in the history of the World Cup.

Argentina's opening goal in the quarter-final was scored by Diego Maradona with his hand. This was clearly visible on television, but the linesman's view was obstructed by Peter Shilton, whose outstretched arm fortuitously eclipsed that of the Argentine striker - from behind the England keeper, Maradona appeared to have won the ball fairly with his head. Maradona then clinched it for Argentina with a run from his own half which cut through the heart of the by no means absent England defence - this was undeniably a good goal in both senses. England rallied and pulled a goal back through Gary Lineker, who later had a chance to bring the scores back level. But Argentina won 2-1.

Afterwards, Maradona said his first goal was 'A little bit the head of Maradona, a little bit the hand of God' - the irony of which has never been much appreciated in England.

Brazil were widely fancied to repeat their 1970 success in the previous Mexico World Cup, but they went out on penalties in the quarter-final to France.

West Germany progressed quietly to the semi-finals, beating Morocco 1-0 and Mexico 4-1 on penalties after their quarter-final finished goalless after extra time.

Belgium progressed by beating the USSR 4-3 and then Spain 5-4 on penalties in the quarter-final after the match had been drawn 1-1.

In the semi-finals, Argentina beat Belgium 2-0 and West Germany beat France 2-0.

The 1986 World Cup Final was held in the Aztec Stadium, Mexico City on June 29, 1986 in front of a crowd of 114,590.

ARGENTINA: Pumpido, Cuciuffo, Brown, Ruggeri, Olarticoechea, Giusti, Batista, Burruchaga (sub: Trubbiani), Enrique, Maradona, Valdano
WEST GERMANY: Schumacher, Berthold, Briegel, Jakobs, Forster, Eder, Brehme, Matthaus, Allofs (sub: Voller), Magath (sub: Hoeness), Rummenigge

Argentina went two up with a first half goal by José Luis Brown and another after 56 minutes by Jorge Valdano. But the Germans clawed their way back to 2-2, with goals by Karl-Heinz Rummenigge and substitute Rudi Voller. Then, six minutes from time, Maradona released Jorge Burruchaga who raced away to leave the final score Argentina 3 West Germany 2.

The leading scorer in the 1986 World Cup finals was England's Gary Lineker, with six goals. Three players scored five - Emilio Butragueno (Spain), Diego Maradona (Argentina) and Careca (Brazil).

During the close season, Everton sold England striker Gary Lineker to Barcelona for £4,262,000. The Spanish club was managed by Terry Venables.

In 1987, Everton won the League Championship for the ninth time.

The leading scorer in the First Division was Clive Allen, with 33 goals in the season for third-placed Tottenham Hotspur.

Coventry City won the 1987 FA Cup, their first major honour since they entered the Football League in 1919. They beat Tottenham Hotspur 3-2 after extra time in the Final, with goals by Dave Bennett and Keith Houchen and an own goal by Spurs' Gary Mabbutt. Mabbutt also played a major part in his own side's second goal, when his shot was deflected in off Coventry defender Brian Kilcline. Spurs had opened the scoring through Clive Allen but had been pulled back to 1-1.

The Littlewoods Cup (as the League Cup was now named, after its new sponsor) was won by Arsenal, who beat Liverpool 2-1 in the Final. Both Gunners Wembley goals were scored by Charlie Nicholas. This was the first match in which Ian Rush had scored for Liverpool and finished on the losing side.

After five years at Old Trafford, Ron Atkinson was sacked as manager of Manchester United on November 6 despite having led the club to two FA Cup triumphs and never finishing lower than fourth in the League. His successor was Aberdeen's title-winning manager Alex Ferguson.

Fulham and Queen's Park Rangers announced plans to merge, but the scheme was rejected by the Football League.

At the end of the season, the English First Division was reduced from 22 to 21 clubs and the Second Division increased from 22 to 23.

The final promotion and relegation places in England were decided for the first time by play-offs. Under the new system, the three teams just below the automatic promotion places played off against each other and against the club that finished just above the automatic relegation positions in the division above.

There was also to be automatic relegation to the Conference for the team finishing bottom of the Fourth Division. The first team to suffer this fate were Lincoln City.

The Scottish Premier Division was increased from 10 clubs to 12 and the First Division reduced from 14 clubs to 12.

Rangers won the Scottish League Championship. This was Graeme Souness's first season as player-manager. He was sent off on his debut, leaving the field at the same time as the victim of his tackle, George McCluskey of Hibernian, was carried off. Rangers lost the match 2-1.

Rangers also won the 1987 League Cup, beating Celtic 2-1 in the Final. This was Souness's first trophy with his new club, but the sweetness of victory was soured by a nasty match in which nine players were booked and Celtic's Mo Johnston was sent off.

Rangers were knocked out of the UEFA Cup in the second round by Borussia Moenchengladbach. Two Rangers players were sent off during the second leg in Germany.

Leading scorer in the Scottish First Division was Brain McClair, with 35 goals for second-placed Celtic.

St Mirren won the Scottish FA Cup for the third time in their history, beating Dundee United 1-0 after extra time in the Final.

Porto won the 1987 European Cup, beating Bayern 1987 Munich 2-1 in the Final in Vienna.

Ajax won the Cup Winners' Cup, beating Lokomotiv Leipzig 1-0 in the Final in Athens.

IFK Gothenburg won the UEFA Cup, beating Dundee United 2-1 on aggregate in the Final. Dundee's disappointment came only four days after their defeat in the Scottish FA Cup Final.

In 1987-88, for the first time, the Football League permitted two substitutes per team per match.

Liverpool won the 1988 Championship in the Football League's centenary year. Manchester United were runners-up.

With 26 goals for the Champions, the First Division's leading scorer was John Aldridge.

After only 11 years in the Football League, Wimbledon won the FA Cup, beating Liverpool 1-0 in the 1988 Final. Lawrie Sanchez scored the winner in the first half and after 61 minutes Dons' keeper Dave Beasant saved a penalty from John Aldridge.

Luton Town won the Littlewoods Cup (formerly the League Cup), beating Arsenal 3-2 in the Final. Much of the credit for capturing their first major trophy went to two-goal Brian Stein.

On October 23, 1987, David Pleat resigned as manager of Tottenham Hotspur after tabloid press allegations about his private life.

On April 9, 1988, at the age of 17 years 240 days, Alan Shearer became the youngest player ever to score a hat-trick in the First Division in Southampton's 4-2 defeat of Arsenal.

On April 14, 1988, Chris Kamara of Swindon Town appeared in court where he was fined £1200 and ordered to pay £250 compensation for causing grievous bodily harm on the field of play to Shrewsbury Town striker Jim Melrose.

Chelsea became the first - and as it turned out, the only - team ever to be relegated from the First Division after a play-off. They lost their top-flight status after finishing 18th and then losing to Middlesbrough, who came third in the Second Division.

In Scotland, Celtic did the double, winning the League Championship for the 35th time and the FA Cup for the 28th time.

The leading scorer in the Scottish Premier Division was Tommy Coyne, with 33 goals for seventh-placed Dundee.

The Scottish League Cup went to Rangers, who beat Aberdeen 5-3 on penalties in the Final after the match ended 3-3 after extra time. This was the first time a major British trophy had been decided by a shoot-out.

Less than a week before this Final, Rangers' player-manager Graeme Souness had been suspended for five matches after his third sending-off in 14 months for fouling Billy Stark of Celtic.

There was more trouble for Rangers in April 1988, when Glasgow Sheriff Court fined England internationals Terry Butcher and Chris Woods for disorderly conduct and a breach of the peace on the field of play. The incident had occurred during an Old Firm match the previous October. Frank McAvennie, the only Celtic player charged, was acquitted. The case against another Rangers and England player, Graham Roberts, was not proven.

The Finals of all three major European Cup competitions in 1988 were decided on penalties.

PSV Eindhoven of Holland won the European Cup, beating Benfica 6-5 on penalties after the Final in Stuttgart had been drawn 0-0.

Mechelen of Belgium won the Cup Winners' Cup in their first ever season in European competition. They beat Ajax 1-0 in the Final in Strasbourg.

Bayer Leverkusen of West Germany won the UEFA Cup, beating Espanol of Spain 3-2 on penalties in front of their home crowd after the scores had finished 3-3 on aggregate over two legs.

The finals of the 1988 European Championship were held in West Germany. The eight qualifying nations were Denmark, England, Holland, Italy, the Republic of Ireland, Spain, the USSR and West Germany.

The Republic of Ireland and England were quickly eliminated after finishing third and fourth respectively in the group that also contained the USSR and Holland.

In the semi-finals, Holland beat the hosts, West Germany 2-1 and the USSR beat Italy 2-0.

Facts

The 1988 European Championship Final between Holland and the USSR was held in the Olympic Stadium, Munich on June 25 in front of 72,308 spectators.

The Dutch won their first major international trophy 2-0 thanks to goals by Marco Van Basten and Ruud Gullit and a penalty save by Hans Van Breukelen.

1989 was the year of the Hillsborough disaster, the worst tragedy in the history of British football. On April 15, 95 spectators were crushed to death and 170 injured shortly before the start of the FA Cup semi-final between Liverpool and Nottingham Forest. The Leppings Lane enclosure became swamped with Liverpool supporters who kept coming in, pressing those at the front up against the fencing which had been erected around the perimeter to prevent pitch invasions. The match kicked off on time and was six minutes old before the authorities realised that the activity behind the goal was not routine unrest but the unfolding of a major disaster.

Arsenal won the League Championship for the first time in 18 years. In the final game of the season, they went to Anfield needing to win by two goals - anything less, and the title would go to Liverpool. And that is exactly what they did, with goals by Alan Smith and Michael Thomas.

League Division One 1988-89 - Top of Final Table

	P	W	D	L	F	A	Pts
Arsenal	38	22	10	6	73	36	76
Liverpool	38	22	10	6	65	28	76

Alan Smith was the First Division's leading scorer, with 23 goals in the season.

In the aftermath of Hillsborough, there were calls for the FA Cup to be held over for a year as a mark of respect to the victims of the tragedy. But eventually the Liverpool v Nottingham Forest semi-final was replayed and won 3-1 by Liverpool, who went on to win the trophy with a 3-2 extra time Final victory over Everton. John Aldridge and Ian Rush (2) scored for Liverpool; both Everton's goals came from substitute Stuart McCall.

Nottingham Forest won the Littlewoods (League) Cup, beating Luton Town 3-1 in the Final with two goals from Nigel Clough (one of them a penalty) and one from Neil Webb. Ray Harford scored for Luton.

After the crowd trouble that had marred the previous season's First/Second Division play-off between Chelsea and Middlesbrough, the format of these games was altered. From now on, only the teams seeking promotion would be involved.

In May, 1989, former Leeds United and England manager Don Revie died after a long battle against motor neurone disease.

On June 7, 1989, Peter Shilton became England's most capped player when he made his 109th appearance against Denmark. The previous record holder, with 108 caps, had been Bobby Moore.

On June 20, Gary Lineker returned to England from Barcelona - where he had moved after the 1986 World Cup finals - when he signed for Tottenham Hotspur.

The Scottish League was restructured again - the Premier Division reverted to 10 clubs and the First Division to 14.

Rangers won the Scottish League Championship and began their sequence of nine titles in a row which equalled Celtic's record achievement of 1966-74. They also took the League Cup, beating Aberdeen 3-2 in the Final.

Joint leading scorers in the Scottish Premier Division were Charlie Nicholas of Aberdeen and Mark McGhee of Celtic, each with 16 goals.

Celtic won the Scottish FA Cup, beating Rangers 1-0 in the Final.

AC Milan won the 1989 European Cup, beating Steua Bucharest 4-0 in the Final in Barcelona.

Barcelona won the Cup Winners' Cup, beating Sampdoria 2-0 in the Final in Berne.

Napoli of Italy beat Stuttgart of West Germany 5-4 on aggregate in the Final of the UEFA Cup.

Lord Justice Peter Taylor's Report on the 1989 Hillsborough disaster was published on January 29, 1990. His findings were severely critical of the squalid condition of many grounds and led directly to the introduction of all-seater stadiums.

In 1990, Liverpool won the League Championship for the 18th time.

The First Division's leading scorer was Gary Lineker, with 24 goals for his new club, Tottenham Hotspur.

Manchester United won the FA Cup for the seventh time, beating Crystal Palace 1-0 in the 1990 Final replay after the first match had been drawn 3-3.

Nottingham Forest retained the Littlewoods (League) Cup, beating Oldham Athletic 1-0 in the 1990 Final with a goal by Nigel Jemson.

Tottenham Hotspur sold England international Chris Waddle to Olympique Marseilles for £4.5 million.

Second Division Oldham were Cup club of the season, reaching both the League Cup Final and the semi-final of the FA Cup. The Lancastrians went 32 matches without defeat on their widely-loathed plastic pitch at Boundary Park.

On May 28, Swindon Town won promotion to the First Division when they beat Sunderland in the play-offs. Less than two weeks later, the club was relegated to the Third Division after admitting a catalogue of financial irregularities since 1985. The club later won an appeal against this demotion, and eventually played the 1990-91 season in the Second Division.

Rangers won the Scottish Championship for the second year in succession. It was a remarkable year for them in another way, too - when they bought Mo Johnston from Nantes in July, the former Celtic striker became the first high-profile Roman Catholic ever to sign for the strongly Protestant Gers.

The leading scorer in the Scottish Premier Division was John Robertson, with 17 goals for Heart of Midlothian.

Aberdeen did a domestic Cup double - they beat Rangers 2-1 after extra time in the Final of the League Cup, then beat Celtic 9-8 on penalties in the FA Cup Final which had remained goalless at the end of extra time.

AC Milan retained the European Cup, beating Benfica 1-0 in the 1990 Final in Vienna.

Sampdoria won the Cup Winners' Cup, beating Anderlecht 2-0 after extra time in the Final in Gothenburg.

The UEFA Cup Final was an all-Italian affair in which Juventus beat Fiorentina 3-1 on aggregate.

The 1990 World Cup finals were held in Italy. The 24 qualifying nations were Argentina, Austria, Belgium, Brazil, Cameroon, Colombia, Costa Rica, Czechoslovakia, Egypt, England, Holland, Italy, the Republic of Ireland, Romania, Scotland, South Korea, Spain, Sweden, the United Arab Emirates, Uruguay, the USA, the USSR, West Germany and Yugoslavia.

England topped their group after drawing 1-1 with the Republic of Ireland, 0-0 with Holland and beating Egypt 1-0.

The Republic of Ireland came second in this group after drawing all three of their games. Holland also qualified for the second round, despite coming third in their group.

Scotland beat Sweden 2-1 in their group, but the loss of their two previous games - 1-0 to Costa Rica and 1-0 to Brazil - condemned them to another early exit from the finals.

The top two teams in each of the six groups of four went through automatically to the second round. They were Belgium, Brazil, Cameroon, Costa Rica, Czechoslovakia, England, Italy, the Republic of Ireland, Romania, Spain, West Germany and Yugoslavia. These 12 countries were joined by the four best third-placed teams - Argentina, Colombia, Holland and Uruguay.

In the second round, the 1990 World Cup finals became a knockout competition. England beat Belgium 1-0 with a goal by David Platt seconds before the referee was about to blow for the end of extra time. The Republic of Ireland beat Romania 5-4 on penalties after the two countries had played out a 0-0 draw.

In the quarter-finals, England took the lead against Cameroon, but later found themselves 2-1 down with eight minutes left in normal time. But Lineker was fouled twice in the area and scored himself from each of the resulting penalties - final score after extra time: England 3 Cameroon 2.

The Republic of Ireland reached the end of the road, losing 1-0 to the host nation, Italy.

The 1990 World Cup semi-finals - Argentina v Italy and West Germany v England - were both decided on penalty shoot-outs after both games ended 1-1 after extra time.

The goals in open play in the West Germany v England game were scored by Andreas Brehme and Gary Lineker. Then Stuart Pearce and Chris Waddle missed their spot kicks and West Germany went forward to the Final.

The 1990 World Cup Final was held in the Stadio Olimpico, Rome, on July 8, 1990, in front of 73,603 spectators.

WEST GERMANY: Iligner, Berthold (sub: Reuter), Kohler, Augenthaler, Buchwald, Brehme, Littbarski, Hassler, Matthaus, Voller, Klinsmann
ARGENTINA: Goycochea, Lorenzo, Serrizuela, Sensini, Ruggeri (sub: Monzoni), Simon, Basualdo, Burruchaga (sub: Calderon), Maradona, Troglio, Dezotti

West Germany won 1-0 with a penalty awarded - probably unjustly - for a foul by Sensini on Voller six minutes from time. Brehme scored from the spot. In the 64th minute, after fouling Klinsmann, Monzon became the first player to be sent off in a World Cup Final. There was but a short time to wait for the second dismissal - two minutes after the penalty, Dezotti was directed to the tunnel after trying to drag the ball away from a timewasting German.

Franz Beckenbauer became the first man ever to have both captained and managed World Cup-winning sides.

Although some matches in the knockout stages of the 1990 World Cup finals were exciting - particularly for supporters of England - many believed that the tournament had been seriously weakened as a spectacle by the paucity of goals - only 115 in 52 matches - and by the high number of cautions (164) and sendings-off (16).

Worst of all was the number of matches that had been decided either by penalties or by penalty shoot-outs. Of the last seven matches, from the quarter finals to the Final, only two had been settled in open play without a goal from the penalty spot.

One of these was the third place play-off, in which Italy beat England 2-1 in normal time.

THE NINETIES

The 1990-91 season was the first in which English clubs other than Liverpool were allowed back into Europe after the ban that had been imposed on them in the wake of the Heysel tragedy on May 29, 1985.

Thus the season started with a note of optimism. The total attendance at League matches on the first day of the season was the highest since the start of 1981-82.

At half time in Everton's first game of the season, goalkeeper Neville Southall refused to go back to the dressing room to discuss tactics. He was fined a week's wages by manager Howard Kendall.

On September 8, York City forward David Longhurst collapsed and died from a heart attack during the match against Lincoln City.

Peter Taylor - Brian Clough's managerial assistant in the great days at Derby County - died on October 5 after a long illness at the age of 62.

Arsenal won their 10th League Championship. Their leading scorer - and the First Division's - was Alan Smith, with 23 goals.

Arsenal won the title despite having had two points deducted from their total after a players' brawl during a League game at Old Trafford. Manchester United were docked one point for their involvement in the same incident. Both clubs were fined £50,000.

Liverpool led the table for much of the season, but were stunned by the resignation of manager Kenny Dalglish on February 22, 1991 after 14 years at the club.

Dalglish announced his decision just after Liverpool had drawn 4-4 with local rivals Everton.

The reasons for Dalglish's departure were not made entirely clear, but he was thought to have become sick of the stress of such a high-profile job. However, there must have been some compensations to being a successful manager of England's most successful club. Leeds United manager Howard Wilkinson expressed the thoughts of many when he said: 'If he has resigned because of pressures, the rest of us have no chance'.

Over the next seven weeks, Liverpool lost the League leadership and saw Arsenal move five points ahead of them at the top of the table. On April 16, the Anfield board announced that Dalglish's successor would be Graeme Souness, their former player who was currently manager of Rangers.

Another famous figure who seemed to have grown tired of the game was rock star Elton John, who in August sold his stake in Watford to Jack Petchey for £6 million.

Former Liverpool and Wales forward John Toshack was sacked as manager of Real Madrid despite the club having suffered only eight defeats during his 64 matches in charge.

During the 1990-91 season, Atletico Madrid goalkeeper Abel Resino went more than 14 matches (1275 minutes) without conceding a goal - a new world record.

On January 1, 1991, Paul Gascoigne became the first player to be sent off on live British television when he got his marching orders for dissent during Tottenham Hotspur's League game against Manchester United.

In recognition of the fact that he had never been booked or sent off in his career, FIFA awarded Gary Lineker their Fair Play prize, worth £20,000.

UEFA announced that, from the start of the 1991-92 season, clubs would be allowed to field up to five foreign players in domestic League games.

Tottenham Hotspur won the FA Cup, beating Nottingham Forest 2-1 after extra time in the 1991 Final. This was the match in which Paul Gascoigne was stretchered off after a quarter of an hour with a serious knee injury after launching a high, illegal tackle on Forest's Garry Parker. Stuart Pearce scored from the resulting free kick, but Spurs equalised through Paul Stewart. The Londoners should have gone ahead when they were awarded a penalty, but Mark Crossley saved Gary Lineker's spot kick. The winner eventually came from a headed own goal by Forest's Des Walker.

The semi-final between Tottenham and Arsenal had been played at Wembley - the first time an FA Cup tie other than the Final had been held at the stadium. Spurs won 3-1 with one goal from Gascoigne and two from Lineker. Arsenal's goal was scored by Alan Smith.

The injured Gascoigne spent the next year in limbo, uncertain of whether he would remain at Spurs or if he would even play again. At the end of the following season, however, he eventually completed his expected £8.5 million transfer to Lazio of Italy.

Sheffield Wednesday won the 1991 League Cup, which had now been renamed the Rumbelows Cup after its new sponsor. They beat Manchester United 1-0 in the Final with a goal by John Sheridan. The victory was particularly sweet for Wednesday manager Ron Atkinson, who had been sacked by United in 1986.

Wednesday also won promotion back from the Second Division, to which they had been relegated at the end of 1989-90.

Torquay United became the first team to win promotion on penalties. Their play-off final against Blackpool ended 2-2 after extra time and the Devon club won the shoot-out 5-4.

Despite losing their manager, Graeme Souness, to Liverpool, Rangers won the Scottish Championship for the third year running. They also won the League Cup, beating Celtic 2-1 after extra time in the Final.

The leading scorer in the Scottish Premier Division was Tommy Coyne, with 18 goals for third-placed Celtic.

Red Star Belgrade won the European Cup, beating Marseille 5-3 on penalties after the Final in Bari, Italy, had finished goalless at the end of extra time.

Manchester United won the 1991 Cup Winners' Cup, beating Barcelona 2-1 in the Final in Rotterdam. Both United's goals were scored by Mark Hughes, who had returned to Old Trafford in 1988 after spending the least successful period of his career with the Spanish club. Barcelona's goal was scored by Dutch international Ronald Koeman.

Manchester United manager Alex Ferguson thus became the second man after Johann Cruyff to manage two Cup Winners' Cup-winning sides, having previously lifted the trophy with Aberdeen.

In another all-Italian UEFA Cup Final, Inter Milan beat Roma 2-1 on aggregate.

Leeds United won the First Division Championship in 1992, the last year before it became the Premiership. This was the third title in their history.

The leading scorer in the First Division was Ian Wright, with 29 goals in the season. Five of them were scored for Crystal Palace; the other 24 came after his mid-season transfer to Arsenal.

Liverpool won the FA Cup for the fifth time, beating Second Division 2-0 in the Final with goals by Michael Thomas and Ian Rush.

In a departure from tradition, this year's FA Cup runners-up went up the steps first. But, owing to a mix-up, Sunderland were mistakenly given the winners' medals.

Cup-winning manager Graeme Souness was just recovering from major heart surgery.

One of the results of the Taylor Report on the Hillsborough disaster was that there could no longer be an infinite number of Cup replays, partly because of the difficulty of organising security and policing at the grounds. Henceforth, if two clubs were still level after extra time in the first replay, ties would be decided by a penalty shoot-out. Manchester United became the first First Division club to go out of the FA Cup on penalties when they lost in the fourth round in 1992 to Southampton.

Manchester United won the League Cup in its second and last year under the aegis of Rumbelows. They beat Nottingham Forest 1-0 in the Final with a goal by Brian McClair.

On February 5, 1992, Newcastle United, languishing near the bottom of the Second Division, sacked manager Ossie Ardiles and appointed Kevin Keegan to replace him.

Seven months after leaving Liverpool, Kenny Dalglish took over as manager of Blackburn Rovers. Under his guidance, Rovers returned to the top flight of English football after a 26-year absence when they beat Leicester City in the Second Division play-off final at Wembley.

In Scotland, Rangers did the double. They won their fourth consecutive Scottish League title and beat Airdrieonians 2-1 in the Final of the FA Cup.

The Premier Division's leading scorer was Ally McCoist, with 34 goals for Rangers.

Hibernian won the League Cup, beating Dunfermline Athletic 2-0 in the Final.

Barcelona won the European Cup, beating Sampdoria 1-0 after extra time in the 1992 Final at Wembley.

Werder Bremen won the Cup Winners' Cup, beating Monaco 2-0 in the Final in Lisbon.

Ajax Amsterdam won the UEFA Cup, beating Torino on away goals after the Final had finished 2-2 on aggregate.

The 1992 European Championships were held in Sweden. The eight competing nations were the CIS (a team representing the new republics of the former USSR), Denmark, England, France, Germany (the old East and West Germany had now been reunified), Holland, Scotland and Sweden.

Denmark appeared in the finals despite having failed to qualify when Yugoslavia were expelled from the tournament because of civil war in the disintegrating federation.

England performed disappointingly, drawing 0-0 with Denmark and France and losing 2-1 to Sweden in the group stage.

In the closing stages of the match against Sweden, England manager Graham Taylor controversially substituted Gary Lineker when the striker needed just one more goal to equal Bobby Charlton's England record of 49. This turned out to be Lineker's last international appearance.

Scotland also went out in the group stage - although they beat the CIS 2-0, they lost 1-0 to Holland and 2-0 to Germany.

In the semi-finals, Germany beat the hosts, Sweden, 3-2. Denmark drew 2-2 with Holland after extra time but went through 5-4 on penalties.

The 1992 European Championship Final was held on June 26, 1992 in Gothenburg in front of a crowd of 37,800. Rank outsiders Denmark beat red-hot favourites Germany 2-0, with goals by John Jensen and Kim Vilfort.

In 1992-93, the Football League disbanded after 104 years and re-formed as the FA Premier League, the first main commercial sponsor of which was Barclays Bank. The Premier League will carry on with 22 clubs for this season, and then reduce its size to 20 by the end of 1994-95. The old Second Division would henceforth be known as the First Division and there would be three-up, three-down between it and the Premiership.

The first FA Premier League Champions were Manchester United.

Alex Ferguson thus became only the third British manager to win a League title with two different clubs - the other two were Herbert Chapman (Huddersfield Town and Arsenal) and Brian Clough (Derby County and Nottingham Forest).

One of the main contributory factors to United's success was their capture of Eric Cantona, who they bought for about £1.5 million on November 26 after the French striker had fallen out with his previous boss, Howard Wilkinson of Leeds United.

Teddy Sheringham was the Premiership's leading scorer, with 22 goals (one for Nottingham Forest, 21 for Tottenham Hotspur).

Arsenal did a Cup double, beating Sheffield Wednesday 2-1 in both Finals. They won the FA Cup, beating the Owls 2-1 in a replay after the first match had finished 1-1 after extra time. Ian Wright scored for Arsenal in both games.

In the Final of the League Cup (which was now known as the Coca-Cola Cup), the Arsenal scorers were Paul Merson and Steve Morrow. Morrow then broke his arm when he fell off Tony Adams during celebrations after the final whistle.

The FA Cup semi-finals were both local derbies - Sheffield Wednesday v Sheffield United and Arsenal v Tottenham Hotspur - and were both played at Wembley.

On February 24, 1993, England's World Cup-winning captain, Bobby Moore, died of cancer at the age of 51.

On May 1, 1993, Brian Clough retired after 18 years as manager of Nottingham Forest. Under him, Forest had won the League Championship in 1978, the European Cup in 1979 and 1980 and the League Cup in 1978, 1979, 1989 and 1990. The only trophy to have eluded Clough throughout his career was the FA Cup.

On May 14, 1993, Terry Venables was sacked as chief executive of Tottenham Hotspur by the club chairman, Alan Sugar.

Kevin Keegan guided Newcastle United to the Championship of the First Division (the old League Division Two).

Maidstone United of Division Three were declared bankrupt and went out of the Football League.

In Scotland, Rangers did the treble. They won their fifth consecutive League title and for the second year running their leading scorer was Ally McCoist, again with 34 goals.

Rangers also won the FA Cup and the League Cup, beating Aberdeen 2-1 in both Finals (the League Cup after extra time).

Olympique Marseille won the 1993 European Cup Final, beating AC Milan 1-0 in Munich, but they were stripped of the title the following year when it emerged that they had fixed a French league fixture against Valenciennes. Their chairman, Bernard Tapie, was charged with corruption and suborning witnesses and ordered to give up ownership of the club. He was subsequently sentenced to two years' imprisonment. The team was relegated to the Second Division.

Parma won the European Cup Winners' Cup, beating Royal Antwerp 3-1 in the Final at Wembley.

Juventus won the UEFA Cup, beating Borussia Dortmund 6-1 on aggregate in the Final.

In 1994, Manchester United did the double. They won the FA Premiership again and beat Chelsea 4-0 in the FA Cup Final thanks to two penalties by Eric Cantona and two goals by Mark Hughes and Brian McClair.

The leading scorer in the Premier League was Andy Cole, with 34 goals for newly-promoted Newcastle United, who finished third.

United nearly did an unprecedented treble, but lost 3-1 to Aston Villa in the Final of the League (Coca-Cola) Cup. Villa's goals in this match were scored by Dalian Atkinson and Dean Saunders (two - one penalty). United's scorer was Mark Hughes.

On January 20, 1994, Sir Matt Busby, president of Manchester United, died at the age of 84.

Graeme Souness resigned as Liverpool manager after his team was knocked out of the FA Cup by First Division Bristol City. He was succeeded by Roy Evans.

The penalties imposed on Tottenham Hotspur for illegal loans to players in the 1980s were unprecedented in their severity - they were fined £1.5 million, banned from the 1994-95 FA Cup and docked six League points. These were later overturned by the English courts.

Wycombe Wanderers took Maidstone United's place in the Football League. They finished fourth in their first season in the Third Division and then won promotion through the play-offs, beating Preston North End in the Final at Wembley.

A week after England's failure to qualify for the 1994 World Cup finals, their much-maligned manager Graham Taylor resigned and the FA announced that his successor would be Terry Venables. The former Tottenham chief executive would be known as coach rather than as manager.

Wales also failed to qualify for the World Cup finals, and this meant the end for their manager, Terry Yorath. His replacement, John Toshack, was taken on part-time so that he could continue in charge of the Spanish club Real Sociedad. This was such an unpopular move that Toshack resigned after only 47 days in charge of the national side.

Facts ⚽

In Scotland, Rangers won the Premier Division for the sixth time in a row and also took the League Cup, beating Hibernian 2-1 in the Final.

Leading scorer in Scotland was Rangers' England international Mark Hateley, with 24 goals.

Dundee United won the FA Cup for the first time in their history, beating Rangers 1-0 in the Final. The Terrors had been losing finalists six times since 1974.

Italians AC Milan won the European Cup, beating Barcelona 4-0 in the Final in Athens.

Arsenal won the Cup Winners' Cup, beating Parma 1-0 in the Final in Copenhagen. The winning goal was scored by Alan Smith.

Inter Milan won the 1994 UEFA Cup, beating Salzburg 2-0 on aggregate in the Final.

The 1994 World Cup finals were held in the USA. The 24 qualifying nations were Argentina, Belgium, Bolivia, Brazil, Bulgaria, Cameroon, Colombia, Germany, Greece, Holland, Italy, Mexico, Morocco, Nigeria, Norway, Republic of Ireland, Romania, Russia, Saudi Arabia, South Korea, Spain, Sweden, Switzerland and the USA.

Andres Escobar, the Colombian defender who scored an own goal in his country's 2-1 defeat by the hosts, was shot dead on his return home.

Diego Maradona failed a random drugs test after Argentina's second match against Nigeria and was sent home in disgrace.

The top two countries in each group went through to the second, knockout, phase. These were Brazil, Bulgaria, Germany, Holland, Mexico, Nigeria, Republic of Ireland, Romania, Saudi Arabia, Spain, Sweden and Switzerland.

They were joined in the knockout stage by the four best third-placed teams - Argentina, Belgium, Italy and the USA.

The Republic of Ireland went through to the second phase after winning one, drawing one and losing one of their three group matches. Their 1-0 victory over Italy came after a shot by Ray Houghton deceived the Italian keeper in the air.

Holland beat the Republic of Ireland 2-0 in the last 16 match at Orlando, Florida.

Germany beat Belgium 3-2 but the result might have been different if the Belgians had not had a penalty turned down by Swiss referee Kurt Rothlisberger. The official admitted his mistake after seeing the video replay and was not used again in the tournament.

Nigeria led for much of their game against Italy, who had Gianfranco Zola sent off. But then in the 88th minute Roberto Baggio equalised and then scored the winner in extra time from the penalty spot.

In the other second phase matches, Spain beat Switzerland 3-0, Sweden beat Saudi Arabia 3-1, Romania beat Argentina 3-2, Brazil beat the USA 1-0 and Bulgaria beat Mexico 5-4 on penalties after the two countries had finished 1-1 after extra time.

In the quarter-finals, Brazil beat Holland 3-2 after throwing away a two-goal lead; Romania went out on penalties for the second World Cup in succession, losing 5-4 to Sweden after a 2-2 draw, and Italy beat Spain 2-1. But the performance of the round was Bulgaria's 2-1 defeat of Germany, who were widely regarded as the holders even though they had won the World Cup in 1990 as West Germany.

Roberto Baggio scored both Italy's goals as they eliminated Bulgaria in one semi-final; in the other, Brazil beat Sweden 1-0 thanks to an 81st minute goal from Romario.

The 1994 World Cup Final was held on July 17 at the Pasadena Rose Bowl, Los Angeles, California, in front of 94,194 spectators.

BRAZIL: Taffarel, Jorginho (sub: Cafu), Aldair, Marcio Santos, Branco, Mauro Silva, Dunga, Mazinho, Zinho (sub: Viola), Babeto, Romario
ITALY: Pagliuca, Mussi (sub: Apolloni), Baresi, Maldini, Benarrivo, Berti, Albertini, D. Baggio (sub: Evani), Donadoni, R. Baggio, Massaro

The Final finished 0-0 after extra time and so for the first time the World Cup was decided on penalties.

Baresi missed the first kick; Pagliuca saved from Marcio Santos; Albertini scored; Romario scored; Evani scored; Branco scored; Taffarel saved the fourth Italian penalty from Massaro; Dunga scored; Roberto Baggio fired over the bar.

Brazil won the 1994 World Cup 3-2 on penalties.

The joint leading scorers in the 1994 World Cup were Salenko of Russia and Stoichkov of Bulgaria, each with six goals.

The tournament was the best-attended of all 15 World Cups, with an average gate of 68,592.

At the start of the 1994-95 season, Tottenham Hotspur swooped on three World Cup stars - Jurgen Klinsmann of Germany and Ilie Dumitrescu and Gica Popescu of Romania. Then, in October, they sacked manager Ossie Ardiles and replaced him with Gerry Francis.

In the close season, Liverpool paid Nottingham Forest £8.5 million for Stan Collymore and Arsenal bought Dennis Bergkamp from Inter Milan for the same amount and then David Platt from Sampdoria for £4.75 million. Manchester United sold Paul Ince to Inter Milan for £7.5 million.

Newcastle United bought Les Ferdinand from Queen's Park Rangers for £6 million, Warren Barton for £4 million from Wimbledon and David Ginola for £2.5 million from Paris St Germain.

Aston Villa bought Gareth Southgate from relegated Crystal Palace for £2.5 million, Savo Milosevic from Partizan Belgrade for £3.5 million, and Mark Draper from Leicester City for the same amount.

Blackburn Rovers won the 1994-95 FA Premier League Championship, finishing a point ahead of Manchester United in second place. This was the third League title in their history, but their first since 1914.

Kenny Dalglish thus joined Herbert Chapman, Brian Clough and Alex Ferguson in the select band of managers who had won a League championship with two clubs.

Everton won the FA Cup for the fifth time, beating Manchester United 1-0 in the 1995 Final through a goal by Paul Rideout.

Liverpool won the Coca-Cola Cup, beating Bolton Wanderers 2-1 in the Final. Steve McManaman scored both Liverpool's goals.

Crystal Palace reached the semi-finals of both the FA and the League (Coca-Cola) Cups and were then relegated form the Premier Division.

Eric Cantona was sent off while playing for Manchester United at Crystal Palace. On his way to the dressing room, the Frenchman attacked a spectator who had been hurling abuse at him.

Cantona was subsequently banned by the FA until the following season and a magistrate sentenced him to two weeks' imprisonment (although the judgment was overturned on appeal, and Cantona had to do 120 hours' community service.

Bruce Grobbelaar (Southampton), John Fashanu (Aston Villa) and Hans Segers (Wimbledon) were charged by the police with match-fixing.

George Graham, manager of Arsenal since 1986, was sacked by the club when a Premier League inquiry revealed that he had received a total of £425,000 in 'bungs' for himself when he signed John Jensen and Pal Lydersen in 1991 and 1992.

Scotland went over for the first time to the three-points-for-a-win system. The Scottish League was also restructured and increased in size from 38 to 40 clubs. From now on, there were to be four divisions, rather than three. The two new clubs were Caledonian Thistle and Ross County.

In 1995, Rangers won their seventh League Championship in a row, the 45th in their history.

After six years without a trophy, Celtic ended the drought when they beat Airdrieonians 1-0 in the Final of the FA Cup. The winning goal was scored by Dutchman Pierre Van Hooijdonk.

The Scottish League Cup was won by Raith Rovers, who beat Celtic 6-5 on penalties after the match had finished 2-2 after extra time. This was the first major trophy in the history of the Kirkcaldy club.

Ajax Amsterdam won the European Cup, beating AC Milan 1-0 in the Final in Vienna.

Zaragoza won the Cup Winners' Cup, beating Arsenal 2-1 after extra time in the Final in Paris. The winning goal came less than a minute before the final whistle would have signalled a penalty shoot-out. Nayim - an ex-Spur whose real name is Mohamed Ali Amar - lifted the ball over Arsenal keeper David Seaman from the halfway line.

In an all-Italian Final, Parma won the UEFA Cup, beating Juventus 2-1 on aggregate.

In December 1995, the European Court of Justice made a historic ruling which had seismic repercussions throughout British and continental football.

The judgment concerned a Belgian player named Jean-Marc Bosman who had signed for RFC Liège in 1988. Two years later, when his contract expired, he was offered a new deal with the club but at less than half his previous wage. He said he would prefer a transfer to Dunkerque, who had expressed an interest in him, but Liège blocked this by putting him on the market at more than twice what Dunkerque were prepared to pay.

Bosman claimed that this was in restraint of trade and the European Court of Justice supported him. In their view, existing football transfer rules were in breach of EEC laws governing free movement of labour within all member states. They also ruled that restrictions on the number of foreign players in a team were likewise unlawful.

As a result of the Bosman Ruling, any player who is out of contract is a free agent, and his present club can no longer expect anything from another club who buys his services. Today, more players than ever before are transferred when they are in the middle of a contract, so that the selling club can make money on the deal.

Manchester United won both the League and the FA Cup for the second time in three years and thus became the first English team ever to do a double double. They won the Premier League with 82 points, four points ahead of second-placed Newcastle United, and beat Liverpool 1-0 in the FA Cup Final with a goal by Eric Cantona.

Premiership leading scorer Alan Shearer of Blackburn Rovers became the first player ever to score more than 30 goals in three consecutive seasons.

Aston Villa won the League (Coca-Cola) Cup, beating Leeds United 3-0 in the Final with goals by Savo Milosevic, Ian Taylor and Dwight Yorke.

Terry Venables announced that he would not continue as England coach after the end of the 1996 European Championships (Euro '96). The FA appointed as his successor Glenn Hoddle, the former Tottenham Hotspur and England player who was currently manager of Chelsea.

First Division Leicester City lost their second manager in less than a year. Aston Villa had taken Brian Little from them in 1994, and in December, 1995, his replacement, Mark McGhee, was poached by Wolverhampton Wanderers. The parting was extremely acrimonious, but the club soon replaced him with Martin O'Neill, who led them to promotion through the play-offs at the end of the 1995-96 season.

Chelsea appointed former Dutch international Ruud Gullit as player-manager in succession to Hoddle.

Bob Paisley died on February 14, 1996 at the age of 77. He was manager of Liverpool from 1974-83, during which time the club won the European Cup three times, the UEFA Cup once, the League Championship six times and the League Cup three times.

In Scotland, Rangers did the double, winning their eighth League Championship in a row and the FA Cup, beating Heart of Midlothian 5-1 in the Final with two goals from Brian Laudrup and three from Gordon Durie.

Aberdeen won the the League Cup, beating Dundee 2-0 in the 1996 Final.

Juventus won the European Cup, beating Ajax 4-2 on penalties after the Final in Rome had been drawn 1-1.

Paris St Germain became the first French club to win the Cup Winners' Cup, beating Rapid Vienna 1-0 in the Final in Brussels.

Bayern Munich won the UEFA Cup, beating Bordeaux 5-1 on aggregate in the 1996 Final.

Euro '96 - the 1996 European Championships - were held in England. There were 16 qualifying nations, twice as many as in Sweden in 1992. They were Bulgaria, the Czech Republic, Croatia, Denmark, England, France, Germany, Holland, Italy, Portugal, Russia, Scotland, Spain, Switzerland and Turkey.

England topped their group, drawing 1-1 with Switzerland and beating Scotland 2-0 and Holland 4-1.

The seven other countries that joined England in the quarter-finals were the Czech Republic, Croatia, France, Germany, Holland, Portugal and Spain.

England were lucky to draw 0-0 with Spain, who had a goal wrongly disallowed for offside. Then keeper David Seaman excelled himself in the penalty shoot-out, which England won 4-2.

In the other three matches, Germany beat Croatia 2-1, France beat Holland 5-4 on penalties after a 0-0 draw, and the Czech Republic beat Portugal 1-0.

Both semi-finals were decided on penalties. England took the lead against Germany after three minutes through Alan Shearer, but Stefan Kuntz equalised after 16. Both sides scored with their first five penalties, and then Gareth Southgate had England's sixth saved. Andreas Moller made no mistake with Germany's reply, to take them through 6-5.

The Czech Republic and France drew 0-0 after extra time, then won the penalty shoot-out 6-5.

The Euro '96 Final was played at Wembley in front of 73,611 spectators. The Czech Republic took the lead after 59 minutes when Karel Poborsky was fouled in the area and Patrik Berger scored from the penalty.

German manager Berti Vogts then brought on Oliver Bierhoff, who brought the scores level after 73 minutes.

Bierhoff scored again after five minutes of extra time - that was the end of the match, because Euro '96 was the first tournament in which the first team to score in extra time won the match - the so-called 'golden goal'.

Manchester United won the FA Carling Premiership in 1996-97 for the fourth time in five years. Their leading scorer, with 19 goals, was the Norwegian Ole Gunnar Solskjaer.

For the second year running, the leading scorer in the Premiership was Alan Shearer, with 25 goals for his new club, Newcastle United.

Chelsea won the FA Cup for the second time in their history. They beat Middlesbrough 2-0 in the Final with goals from Roberto Di Matteo and Eddie Newton.

Di Matteo's goal was the fastest in Cup Final history - he scored after only 43 seconds, thus beating the previous record set by Jackie Milburn, who scored after 45 seconds of the 1955 Cup Final for Newcastle United against Manchester City.

Leicester City won the League (Coca-Cola Cup), beating Middlesbrough 1-0 in the Final replay at Hillsborough with a goal by Steve Claridge.

Giantkillers of the year were Second Division Chesterfield, who reached the semi-final of the FA Cup.

The Wembley Coca-Cola Cup Final had ended 1-1 after extra time. Emile Heskey scored for Leicester and Fabrizio Ravanelli for Middlesbrough.

Middlesbrough achieved a unique and unwanted treble - they were beaten finalists in both Cups and were relegated from the Premiership. They would have avoided the drop had they not had three points deducted for cancelling a Premiership fixture against Blackburn Rovers without sufficient notice.

Kevin Keegan left his job as manager of Newcastle United in mid-season when his team were second in the Premiership. The club announced plans to become a public company and then, on January 14, 1997, appointed Kenny Dalglish as manager.

After eight years in charge, Howard Wilkinson was sacked as manager of Leeds United. He was later appointed Technical Director of the FA.

Former Arsenal manager George Graham replaced Howard Wilkinson at Elland Road after 18 months out of the game.

Macclesfield Town won the GM Vauxhall Conference and gained entry to the Football league for the first time. Their manager was former Manchester United and Northern Ireland international Sammy McIlroy.

Queen's Park Rangers were bought by music entrepreneur Chris Wright for £10 million.

Former England coach Terry Venables became Director of Football at First Division Portsmouth. He later also took on a part-time job as manager of Australia.

Bruce Rioch was sacked as Arsenal manager after 61 weeks in the job. His replacement was Arsène Wenger, a Frenchman who had previously been coach at Grampus Eight in Japan.

In August 1996, Alan Ball resigned as manager of Manchester City. Six weeks later, the Maine Road board announced his replacement - Steve Coppell, formerly manager of Crystal Palace. Coppell lasted 33 days before resigning 'for health reasons'. He was replaced in December by Frank Clark, who had been manager of Nottingham Forest since 1993.

In Guatemala, 80 people were killed at a football match due to overcrowding in a stadium.

Chelsea director Matthew Harding was killed in a helicopter crash on his way back from watching his team's Coca-Cola Cup match at Bolton Wanderers.

Ray Harford resigned as manager of Blackburn Rovers. The club then announced that his replacement next season would be Sven Goran Eriksson, but he never came and they hired Roy Hodgson instead.

On December 22, 1996, Peter Shilton made his 1000th League appearance for Third Division Leyton Orient.

In Scotland, Rangers won the Premier League for the ninth year in succession, thus equalling Celtic's record of 1966-1974. They also won the League Cup, beating Heart of Midlothian 4-3 in the Final.

Kilmarnock won the 1997 Scottish FA Cup for the third time in their history, beating Falkirk 1-0 in the Final.

Alex Miller resigned as manager of Hibernian after 10 years in charge.

Borussia Dortmund won the European Cup, beating Juventus 3-1 in the Final in Munich.

Barcelona won the Cup Winners' Cup, beating Paris St Germain 1-0 in the Final in Rotterdam.

Schalke won the UEFA Cup, beating Inter Milan 4-1 on penalties after the Final had finished 1-1 on aggregate.

Arsenal won the FA Carling Premiership in 1997-98 - this was the 11th title in their history.

Frenchman Arsène Wenger thus became the first non-British manager to win the English League.

Arsenal completed the Double by winning the FA Cup, beating Newcastle United 2-0 in the Final at Wembley.

Arsenal's goals in the Final were scored by Marc Overmars and Nicolas Anelka.

The Premiership's leading scorer was Andy Cole, with 25 goals in all competitions.

Aston Villa sold controversial and disaffected Yugoslav striker Savo Milosevic to Real Zaragoza for a reported £3.5 million.

Chelsea won the League (Coca-Cola Cup), beating First Division Middlesbrough 2-0 in the Final with goals by Frank Sinclair and Roberto di Matteo.

All three of the clubs promoted to the Premiership at the end of the 1997 season were relegated from it again at the end of 1998 - Bolton Wanderers, Barnsley and Crystal Palace.

Crystal Palace let themselves down badly at home, where they won only one game. This was against Sheffield Wednesday, the only team from whom they took six points in the season.

Everton flirted dangerously with relegation and only ensured safety through a 1-1 draw with Coventry City on the last day of the season.

Promoted automatically from the Nationwide Division One were Nottingham Forest (Champions) and Middlesbrough.

They were joined in the Premiership by Charlton who beat Sunderland 7-6 on penalties after the play-off Final at Wembley had ended 4-4 after extra time. Clive Mendonca scored a hat trick for Charlton in this match.

Kevin Phillips scored one of Sunderland's Wembley goals. It was his 35th of the season, making him the club's all-time leading marksman.

The crucial penalty was taken by Sunderland's Michael Gray and saved by Charlton keeper Sasa Ilic.

Celtic won the Scottish Premier League - their first championship since 1988. Their manager, Wim Jansen, then resigned, it is thought because of disagreements with club chairman Fergus McCann.

Tom Boyd became the first Celtic captain to lift the Premier League trophy for 10 years.

Heart of Midlothian won the Scottish FA Cup, beating Rangers 2-1 in the Final with goals by Colin Cameron (penalty) and Stephane Adam. Ally McCoist scored for Rangers.

Celtic won the Scottish League Cup, beating Dundee United 3-0 in the Final. Their goals were scored by Marc Rieper, Henrik Larsson and Craig Burley.

This was the first season since 1986 that Rangers had failed to win any of the major domestic trophies.

Real Madrid won the European Cup, beating Juventus 1-0 in the Final in the new Amsterdam ArenA. The winning goal was scored after 67 minutes by Montenegran international Predrag Mijatovic.

This was Real's seventh European Cup triumph, but their first since 1966.

Real's German coach, Jupp Heynckes, was thought to be in imminent danger of losing his job.

Chelsea won the 1998 Cup Winners' Cup, beating Stuttgart 1-0 in the Final in Stockholm. The only goal of the game was scored by substitute Gianfranco Zola.

This was the eighth time that a club from England had won the trophy - more than any other nation.

Chelsea's Gianluca Vialli became the first player-manager to win a major European trophy.

Two players were sent off in the Cup Winners' Cup Final - Dan Petrescu of Chelsea and Gerhard Poschner of Stuttgart.

For the first time since 1965, the UEFA Cup Final was a one-off, rather than a two-legged affair. Inter Milan beat Lazio 3-0 in the Parc des Princes, Paris, with goals by Zamorano, Zanetti and Ronaldo.

In the close season it was announced that outgoing Rangers manager Walter Smith would take over at Everton the following season. Smith had been thought to have wanted a rest.

THE 1998
WORLD CUP

The 1998 World Cup finals were held in France, which thus became the second country to host the tournament twice (the other was Mexico in 1970 and 1986). The French had previously hosted the tournament in 1938.

There were 32 finalists, as follows: Argentina, Austria, Belgium, Brazil, Bulgaria, Cameroon, Chile, Colombia, Croatia, Denmark, England, France, Germany, Holland, Iran, Italy, Jamaica, Japan, Mexico, Morocco, Nigeria, Norway, Paraguay, Romania, Saudi Arabia, Scotland, South Africa, South Korea, Spain, Tunisia, the United States and Yugoslavia.

Matches were played in 10 centres across the country. There were two stadia in Paris - the existing Parc des Princes and the new Stade de France at St Denis on the western edge of the city centre. Other venues were Bordeaux, Lens, Lyons, Marseilles, Montpellier, Nantes, Saint-Etienne and Toulouse.

The countries were divided into eight groups, each of four teams. When the draw was made, there were eight top seeds, eight second seeds, eight third seeds and eight fourth seeds.

The eight top seeds were Argentina, Brazil (the holders), France, Germany, Holland, Italy, Romania and Spain.

England had only a moderate build-up to the finals, losing to Chile and drawing with Saudi Arabia and Belgium. The only real source of encouragement was a win over Portugal.

In the run-up to the finals, Scotland drew three and lost two of their try-out games.

The squads of each participating nation were as follows:

Group A

Brazil		Scotland	
1	Taffarel	1	Jim Leighton
2	Cafu	2	Jackie Mcnamara
3	Aldair	3	Tommy Boyd
4	Junior Baiano	4	Colin Calderwood
5	Cesar Sampaio	5	Colin Hendry
6	Roberto Carlos	6	Tosh McKinlay
7	Giovanni	7	Kevin Gallacher
8	Dunga	8	Craig Burley
9	Ronaldo	9	Gordon Durie
10	Rivaldo	10	Darren Jackson
11	Emerson Ferreira	11	John Collins
12	Carlos Germano	12	Neil Sullivan
13	Ze Roberto	13	Simon Donnelly
14	Goncalves	14	Paul Lambert
15	Andre Cruz	15	Scott Gemmill
16	Ze Roberto	16	David Weir
17	Doriva	17	Billy McKinlay
18	Leonardo	18	Matt Elliott
19	Denilson	19	Derek Whyte
20	Bebeto	20	Scott Booth
21	Edmundo	21	Jonathan Gould
22	Dida	22	Christian Dailly
Coach:	Mario Zagalo	Coach:	Craig Brown

Facts

Group A

Norway		Morocco	
I	Frode Grodas	I	**Abdelkader El Brazi**
2	Gunnar Halle	2	**Abdelilah Saber**
3	Ronny Johnsen	3	**Abdelkrim El Hadrioui**
4	Henning Berg	4	**Youssef Rossi**
5	Stig Inge Bjornebye	5	**Smahi Triki**
6	Stale Solbakken	6	**Noureddine Naybet**
7	Erik Mykland	7	**Mustapha Hadji**
8	Oyvind Leonhardsen	8	**Said Chiba**
9	Tore Andre Flo	9	**Abdeljalil Hadda**
10	Kjetil Rekdal	10	**Abderrahim Ouakili**
11	Jahn Ivar Jakobsen	11	**Ali El Khattabi**
12	Thomas Myhre	12	**Driss Benzekri**
13	Espen Baardsen	13	**Rachid Nehrouz**
14	Vegard Heggem	14	**Salaheddine Bassir**
15	Dan Eggen	15	**Lahcen Abrami**
16	Jostein Flo	16	**Rachid Azzouzi**
17	Havard Flo	17	**Gharib Amzine**
18	Egil Ostenstad	18	**Youssef Chippo**
19	Erik Hoftun	19	**Jamal Sellami**
20	Ole Gunnar Solskjaer	20	**Taher El Lakhlej**
21	Vidar Riseth	21	**Rachid Roki**
22	Roar Strand	22	**Mustapha Chadli**
Coach:	Egil Olsen	Coach:	**Henri Michel**

Group B

Italy		Chile	
1	Francesco Toldo	1	Nelson Tapia
2	Guiseppe Bergomi	2	Cristian Castaneda
3	Paolo Maldini	3	Ronaldo Fuentes
4	Fabio Cannavaro	4	Francisco Rojas
5	Alessandro Costacurta	5	Javier Margas
6	Alessandro Nesta	6	Pedro Reyes
7	Gianluca Pessotto	7	Nelson Parraguez
8	Moreno Torricelli	8	Clarence Acuna
9	Demetrio Albertini	9	Ivan Zamorano
10	Allesandro Del Piero	10	Jose Luis Sierra
11	Dino Baggio	11	Marcelo Salas
12	Gianluca Pagliuca	12	Marcelo Ramirez
13	Allesandro Cois	13	Manuel Neira
14	Luigi Di Biagio	14	Miguel Ramirez
15	Angelo Di Livio	15	Moises Villarroel
16	Roberto Di Matteo	16	Mauricio Aros
17	Francesco Moriero	17	Marcelo Vega
18	Roberto Baggio	18	Luis Musrri
19	Filippo Inzaghi	19	Fernando Cornejo
20	Fabrizio Ravanelli	20	Fabian Estay
21	Christian Vieri	21	Rodrigo Barrera
22	Gianluigi Buffon	22	Carlos Tejas
Coach:	Cesare Maldini	Coach:	Nelson Acosta

Group B

Cameroon		Austria	
1	Jacques Songo'o	1	**Michael Konsel**
2	Joseph Elanga	2	**Markus Schopp**
3	Pierre Wome	3	**Peter Schottel**
4	Rigobert Song	4	**Anton Pfeffer**
5	Raymond Kalla Nkongo	5	**Wolfgang Feiersinger**
6	Pierre Njanka	6	**Walter Kogler**
7	François Omam-Biyick	7	**Mario Haas**
8	Didier Angibeaud	8	**Heimo Pfeifenberger**
9	Alphonse Tchami	9	**Ivica Vastic**
10	Patrick Mboma	10	**Andreas Herzog**
11	Samule Eto'o	11	**Martin Amerhauser**
12	Jean-Jacques Etame	12	**Martin Hiden**
13	Serge Kwetche	13	**Harald Cerny**
14	Augustine Simo	14	**Hannes Reinmayer**
15	Joseph Ndo	15	**Arnold Wetl**
16	William Andem	16	**Franz Wohlfahrt**
17	Michel Pensee	17	**Roman Mahlich**
18	Samuel Ipoua	18	**Peter Stoger**
19	Marcel Mahouve	19	**Toni Polster**
20	Salomon Olembe	20	**Andreas Heraf**
21	Joseph-Desire Job	21	**Wolfgang Knaller**
22	Alioum Boukar	22	**Dietmar Kuhbauer**
Coach:	Claude Le Roy	Coach:	**Herbert Prohaska**

Group C

France		Denmark	
1	Bernard Lama	1	Peter Schmeichel
2	Vincent Candela	2	Michael Schjonberg
3	Bixente Lizarazu	3	Marc Rieper
4	Patrick Vieira	4	Jes Hogh
5	Laurent Blanc	5	Jan Heintze
6	Youri Djorkaeff	6	Thomas Helveg
7	Didier Deschamps	7	Allan Neilsen
8	Marcel Desailly	8	Per Frandsen
9	Stephane Guivarc'h	9	Miklos Molnar
10	Zindine Zidane	10	Michael Laudrup
11	Robert Pires	11	Brian Laudrup
12	Thierry Henry	12	Soren Colding
13	Bernard Diomede	13	Jacob Laursen
14	Alain Boghossian	14	Morten Wieghorst
15	Lilian Thuram	15	Stig Tofting
16	Fabien Barthez	16	Mogens Krogh
17	Emmanuel Petit	17	Bjarne Goldbaek
18	Frank Lebouef	18	Peter Moller
19	Christian Karembeu	19	Ebbe Sand
20	David Trezeguet	20	Rene Henriksen
21	Christophe Dugarry	21	Martin Jorgensen
22	Lionel Charbonnier	22	Peter Kjaer
Coach:	Aime Jacquet	Coach:	Bo Johansson

The 1998 World Cup

Facts

Group C

	South Africa		Saudi Arabia
1	Hans Vonk	1	Mohammed Al-Deayea
2	Themba Mnguni	2	Mohammed Al-Jahani
3	David Nyathi	3	Mohammed Al-Khilaiwi
4	Willem Jackson	4	Abdullah Zubramwi
5	Mark Fish	5	Ahmed Madani
6	Phil Masinga	6	Fuad Amin
7	Quinton Fortune	7	Ibrahim Al-Shahrani
8	Alfred Phiri	8	Obeid Al-Dosari
9	Shaun Bartlett	9	Sami Al-Jaber
10	John Moshoeu	10	Saeed Al-Owairan
11	Helman Mkhalele	11	Fahd Al-Mehallel
12	Brendan Augustine	12	Ibrahim Al-Harbi
13	Delron Buckley	13	Hussain Sulimani
14	Jerry Sikhosana	14	Khalid Al-Muwalid
15	Doctor Khumalo	15	Youssef Al-Thyniyan
16	Brian Baloyi	16	Khamis Al-Owairan
17	Benni McCarthy	17	Ahmed Al-Dosari
18	Lebogang Morula	18	Nawaf Al-Temiyat
19	Lucas Radebe	19	Abdel Aziz Al-Janoubi
20	Naughty Mokoena	20	Hamza Saleh
21	Pierre Issa	21	Hussein Al-Sadiq
22	Andre Arendse	22	Tisir Al-Antarif

Coach: Philippe Troussier

Coach: Carlos Alberto Parreira

Group D

Spain		Nigeria	
1	Andoni Zubizarreta	1	**Peter Rufai**
2	Albert Ferrer	2	**Jero Shakpoke**
3	Agustin Aranzabal	3	**Celestine Babayaro**
4	Rafael Alkorta	4	**Nwankwo Kanu**
5	Abelardo	5	**Uche Okechukwu**
6	Fernando Hierro	6	**Taribo West**
7	Fernando Morientes	7	**Finidi George**
8	Julen Guerrero	8	**Mutiu Adepoju**
9	Juan Pizzi	9	**Rashidi Yekini**
10	Raul Gonzalez	10	**Jay-Jay Okocha**
11	Alfonso Perez	11	**Garba Lawal**
12	Sergi Barjuan	12	**Willy Okpara**
13	Santiago Canizares	13	**Tijani Babangida**
14	Ivan Campo	14	**Daniel Amokachi**
15	Carlos Aguilera	15	**Sunday Oliseh**
16	Alberto Celades	16	**Uche Okafor**
17	Joseba Etxeberria	17	**Augustine Eguavoen**
18	Guillermo Amor	18	**Wilson Oruma**
19	Narvaez Kiko	19	**Ben Iroha**
20	Miguel Nadal	20	**Victor Ikpeba**
21	Luis Enrique Martinex	21	**Godwin Okpara**
22	Jose Molina	22	**Abiodun Baruwa**
Coach:	Javier Clemente	Coach:	**Bora Milutinovic**

Group D

Paraguay

1 Jose Chilavert
2 Francisco Arce
3 Catalino Rivarola
4 Carlos Gamarra
5 Celso Ayala
6 Edgar Aguilera
7 Juan Carlos Yegros
8 Aristides Rojas
9 Jose Cardozo
10 Roberto Acuna
11 Pedro Sarabia
12 Danilo Aceval
13 Carlos Paredes
14 Ricardo Rojas
15 Miguel Benitez
16 Julio Cesar Enciso
17 Hugo Brizuela
18 Cesar Ramirez
19 Carlos Morales
20 Denis Caniza
21 Jorge Campos
22 Ruben Ruiz Diaz
Coach: Paulo Cesar
           Carpeggiani

Bulgaria

1 Zdravko Zdravkov
2 Radostin Kisishev
3 Trifon Ivanov
4 Ivailo Petkov
5 Ivailo Iordanov
6 Zlatko Yankov
7 Emil Kostadinov
8 Hristo Stoichkov
9 Luboslav Penev
10 Krassimir Balakov
11 Ilian Iliev
12 Borislav Mihailov
13 Gosho Ginchev
14 Marian Hristov
15 Adalbert Zafirov
16 Anatoli Nankov
17 Stoicho Stoilov
18 Daniel Borimirov
19 Georgi Bachev
20 Georgi Kirilov
21 Rosen Kirilov
22 Milen Petkov
Coach: Hristo Bonev

Group E

Netherlands		Belgium	
1	Edwin van der Sar	1	**Filip de Wilde**
2	Michael Reiziger	2	**Bertrand Crasson**
3	Jaap Stam	3	**Lorenzo Staelens**
4	Frank de Boer	4	**Gordan Vidovic**
5	Arthur Numan	5	**Vital Borkelmans**
6	Wim Jonk	6	**Franky van der Elst**
7	Ronald de Boer	7	**Marc Wilmots**
8	Dennis Bergkamp	8	**Luis Oliveira**
9	Patrick Kluivert	9	**Mbo Mpenza**
10	Clarence Seedorf	10	**Luc Nilis**
11	Phillip Cocu	11	**Nico van Kerckhoven**
12	Boudewijn Zenden	12	**Philippe van de Walle**
13	Andre Ooijer	13	**Dany Verlinden**
14	Marc Overmars	14	**Enzo Scifo**
15	Winston Bogarde	15	**Philippe Clement**
16	Edgar Davids	16	**Glen de Boeck**
17	Pierre van Hooijdonk	17	**Mike Vestraeten**
18	Ed de Goey	18	**Gert Verheyen**
19	Giovanni van Bronckhorst	19	**Eric van Meir**
20	Aron Winter	20	**Emile Mpenza**
21	Jimmy Floyd Hasselbaink	21	**Danny Boffin**
22	Ruud Hesp	22	**Eric Deflandre**
Coach:	Guus Hiddink	Coach:	**Georges Leekens**

Group E

South Korea		Mexico	
1	Kim Byung-ji	1	Jorge Campos
2	Choi Sung-yong	2	Claudio Suarez
3	Lee Lim-saeng	3	Joel Sanchez
4	Choi Young-il	4	German Villa
5	Lee Min-sung		Castenada
6	Yoo Sang-chul	5	Diulio Davino
7	Kim Doh-keun	6	Marcelino Bernal
8	Noh Jung-yoon	7	Ramon Ramirez
9	Kim Do-hoon	8	Alberto Garcia Aspe
10	Choi Yong-soo	9	Ricardo Pelaez
11	Seo Jung-won	10	Luis Garcia
12	Lee Sang-hun	11	Cuauhtemoc Blanco
13	Kim Tae-young	12	Osvaldo Sanchez
14	Ko Jong-soo	13	Pavel Pardo
15	Lee Sang-yoon	14	Raul Lara
16	Jang Hyung-seok	15	Luis Hernandez
17	Ha Seok-ju	16	Isaac Terrazas
18	Hwang Sun-hong	17	Francisco Palencia
19	Jang Dae il	18	Salvador Carmona
20	Hong Myung-bo	19	Braulio Luna
21	Lee Dong-gook	20	Jaime Ordiales
22	Seo Dong-myung	21	Jesus Arellano
Coach:	Cha Bum-kun	22	Oscar Perez
		Coach:	Manuel Lapuente

Group F

Germany		Yugoslavia	
1	Andreas Kopke	1	**Ivica Kralj**
2	Christian Worns	2	**Zoran Mirkovic**
3	Jorg Heinrich	3	**Goran Djorovic**
4	Jurgen Kohler	4	**Slavisa Jokanovic**
5	Thomas Helmer	5	**Miroslav Djukic**
6	Olaf Thon	6	**Branko Brnovic**
7	Andreas Moller	7	**Vladimir Jugovic**
8	Lothar Matthaus	8	**Dejan Savicevic**
9	Ulf Kirsten	9	**Predrag Mijatovic**
10	Thomas Hassler	10	**Dragan Stojkovic**
11	Olaf Marschall	11	**Sinisa Mihajlovic**
12	Oliver Kahn	12	**Dragoje Lekovic**
13	Jens Jeremies	13	**Slobodan Komljenovic**
14	Markus Babbel	14	**Nisa Saveljic**
15	Steffen Freund	15	**Ljubinko Drulovic**
16	Dietmar Hamann	16	**Zeljko Petrovic**
17	Christian Ziege	17	**Savo Milosevic**
18	Jurgen Klinsmann	18	**Dejan Govedarica**
19	Stefan Reuter	19	**Miroslav Stevic**
20	Oliver Bierhoff	20	**Dejan Stankovic**
21	Michael Tarnat	21	**Perica Ognjenovic**
22	Jens Lehmann	22	**Darko Kovacevic**
Coach:	Berti Vogts	Coach:	**Slobadan Santrac**

Group F

The USA		Iran	
1	Brad Friedel	1	**Ahmadreza Abedzadeh**
2	Frankie Hejduk	2	**Mehdi Mahdavikia**
3	Eddie Pope	3	**Naeem Saadavi**
4	Mike Burns	4	**Mohammad Khakpour**
5	Thomas Dooley	5	**Mohammad Ali**
6	David Regis		**Peyrovani**
7	Roy Wegerle	6	**Karim Bagheri**
8	Ernie Stewart	7	**Alireza Mansourian**
9	Joe-Max Moore	8	**Sirous**
10	Tab Ramos		**Deenmohammadi**
11	Eric Wynalda	9	**Hamid Estili**
12	Jeff Agoos	10	**Ali Daei**
13	Cobi Jones	11	**Khodadad Azizi**
14	Preki Radosavljevic	12	**Nima Nakisa**
15	Chad Deering	13	**Ali Latifi**
16	Jurgen Sommer	14	**Nader**
17	Marcelo Balboa		**Mohammadkhani**
18	Kasey Keller	15	**Ali Ostadasadli**
19	Brian Maisonneuve	16	**Reza Shahroudi**
20	Brian McBride	17	**Javad Zarrincheh**
21	Claudio Reyna	18	**Satar Hamedani**
22	Alexi Lalas	19	**Behnam Seraj**
Coach:	Steve Sampson	20	**Mehdi Pashazadeh**
		21	**Mehrdad Minavand**
		22	**Parviz Boromand**
		Coach:	**Jalal Talebi**

Group G

Romania

1	Dumitru Stingaciu
2	Dan Petrescu
3	Christian Dulca
4	Anton Dobos
5	Constantin Galca
6	Gheorge Popescu
7	Marius Lacatus
8	Dorinel Munteanu
9	Viorel Moldovan
10	Gheorge Hagi
11	Adrian Ilie
12	Bogdan Stelea
13	Liviu Ciobotariu
14	Radu Niculescu
15	Lucian Marinescu
16	Gabriel Popescu
17	Ilie Dumitrescu
18	Iulian Filipescu
19	Ovidiu Stinga
20	Tibor Selymes
21	Gheorge Craioveanu
22	Florian Prunea

Coach: Anghel Iordanescu

Colombia

1	Oscar Cordoba
2	Ivan Ramiro Cordoba
3	Ever Palacios
4	Jose Santa
5	Jorge Bermudez
6	Maurizio Serna
7	Antony de Avila
8	Harold Lozano
9	Adolfo Valencia
10	Carlos Valderrama
11	Faustino Asprilla
12	Miguel Calero
13	Wilmer Calero
14	Jorge Bolano
15	Victor Aristizabal
16	Antonio Moreno
17	Andres Estrada
18	John Perez
19	Freddy Rincon
20	Hamilton Ricard
21	Leider Preciado
22	Farid Mondragon

Coach: Hernan Dario Gomez

Group G

England		Tunisia	
1	David Seaman	1	**Chokri el Ouaer**
2	Sol Campbell	2	**Imed Ben Younes**
3	Graeme Le Saux	3	**Sami Trabelsi**
4	Paul Ince	4	**Mounir Boukadida**
5	Tony Adams	5	**Hatem Trabelsi**
6	Gareth Southgate	6	**Ferid Chouchane**
7	David Beckham	7	**Tarek Thabet**
8	David Batty	8	**Zoubeir Beya**
9	Alan Shearer	9	**Riadh Jelassi**
10	Teddy Sheringham	10	**Kaies Ghodbane**
11	Steve McManaman	11	**Adel Sellimi**
12	Gary Neville	12	**Mourad Melki**
13	Nigel Martyn	13	**Riadh Bouazizi**
14	Darren Anderton	14	**Sirajeddine Chihi**
15	Paul Merson	15	**Skander Souyah**
16	Paul Scholes	16	**Radhouane Salhi**
17	Robert Lee	17	**Jose Clayton**
18	Martin Keown	18	**Mehdi Ben Slimane**
19	Les Ferdinand	19	**Faycal Ben Ahmed**
20	Michael Owen	20	**Sabri Jaballah**
21	Rio Ferdinand	21	**Khaled Badra**
22	Tim Flowers	22	**Ali Boumnijel**
Coach:	Glenn Hoddle	Coach:	**Henry Kasperczak**

Group H

	Argentina			Croatia
1	CArlos Roa		1	**Drazen Ladic**
2	Roberto Ayala		2	**Petar Krpan**
3	Jose Chamot		3	**Ante Seric**
4	Hector Pineda		4	**Igor Stimac**
5	Matias Almeyda		5	**Goran Juric**
6	Nestor Sensini		6	**Slaven Bilic**
7	Claudio Lopez		7	**Aljosa Asanovic**
8	Diego Simeone		8	**Robert Prosinecki**
9	Gabriel Batistuta		9	**Davor Suker**
10	Ariel Ortega		10	**Zvonimir Boban**
11	Juan Veron		11	**Silvio Maric**
12	German Burgos		12	**Marijan Mrmic**
13	Pablo Paz		13	**Mario Stanic**
14	Nelson Vivas		14	**Zvonimir Soldo**
15	Leonardo Astrada		15	**Igor Tudor**
16	Sergio Berti		16	**Ardijan Kozniku**
17	Pablo Cavallero		17	**Robert Jarni**
18	Abel Balbo		18	**Zoran Mamic**
19	Hernan Crespo		19	**Goran Vlaovic**
20	Marcelo Gallardo		20	**Dario Simic**
21	Marcelo Delgado		21	**Krunoslav Jurcic**
22	Javier Zanetti		22	**Vladimir Vasilj**
Coach:	Daniel Passarella		Coach:	**Miroslav Blazevic**

Facts

Group H

Japan		Jamaica	
1	Nobuyuki Kojima	1	**Warren Barrett**
2	Akira Narahashi	2	**Steven Malcolm**
3	Naoki Soma	3	**Christopher Dawes**
4	Masami Ihara	4	**Linval Dixon**
5	Norio Omura	5	**Ian Goodison**
6	Motohiro Yamaguchi	6	**Fitzroy Simpson**
7	Teruyoshi Ito	7	**Peter Cargill**
8	Hidetoshi Nakata	8	**Marcus Gayle**
9	Masashi Nakayama	9	**Andy Williams**
10	Hiroshi Nanami	10	**Walter Boyd**
11	Shinji Ono	11	**Theodore Whitmore**
12	Wagner Lopes	12	**Dean Sewell**
13	Toshihiro Hattori	13	**Aaron Lawrence**
14	Masayuki Okano	14	**Donovan Ricketts**
15	Hiroaki Morishima	15	**Ricardo Gardner**
16	Toshihide Saito	16	**Robbie Earle**
17	Yutaka Akita	17	**Onandi Lowe**
18	Shoji Jo	18	**Deon Burton**
19	Eisuke Nakanishi	19	**Frank Sinclair**
20	Yoshikatsu Kawaguchi	20	**Darryl Powell**
21	Seigo Narazaki	21	**Durrant Brown**
22	Takashi Hirano	22	**Paul Hall**
Coach:	Takeshi Okada	**Coach:**	**Rene Simoes**

The final tables of each group were as follows:

	P	W	D	L	F	A	Pts
Group A							
Brazil	3	2	0	1	6	3	6
Norway	3	1	2	0	5	4	5
Morocco	3	1	1	1	5	5	4
Scotland	3	0	1	2	2	6	1
Group B							
Italy	3	2	1	0	7	3	7
Chile	3	0	3	0	4	4	3
Austria	3	0	2	1	3	4	2
Cameroon	3	0	2	1	2	5	2
Group C							
France	3	3	0	0	9	1	9
Denmark	3	1	1	1	3	3	4
South Africa	3	0	2	1	3	6	2
Saudi Arabia	3	0	1	2	2	7	1
Group D							
Nigeria	3	2	0	1	5	5	6
Paraguay	3	1	2	0	3	1	5
Spain	3	1	1	1	8	4	4
Bulgaria	3	0	1	2	1	7	1
Group E							
Holland	3	1	2	0	7	2	5
Mexico	3	1	2	0	7	5	5
Belgium	3	0	3	0	3	3	3
South Korea	3	0	1	2	2	9	1

The 1998 World Cup

Facts ⚽

	P	W	D	L	F	A	Pts
Group F							
Germany	3	2	1	0	6	2	7
Yugoslavia	3	2	1	0	4	2	7
Iran	3	1	0	2	2	4	3
USA	3	0	0	3	1	5	0
Group G							
Romania	3	2	1	0	4	2	7
England	3	2	0	1	5	2	6
Colombia	3	1	0	2	1	3	3
Tunisia	3	0	1	2	1	4	1
Group H							
Argentina	3	3	0	0	7	0	9
Croatia	3	2	0	1	4	2	6
Jamaica	3	1	0	2	3	9	3
Japan	3	0	0	3	1	4	0

Scotland played in the opening match of the tournament against the holders, Brazil. The champions went ahead after four minutes through Cesar Sampaio, but Scotland got back on terms through a penalty by John Collins. The Scots were unlucky to lose through an own goal when an attempted clearance bounced in off Boyd.

England began their campaign with a 2-0 victory over Tunisia. Their first came from captain Alan Shearer after 42 minutes, the second from Paul Scholes in injury time.

Scotland drew their second game against Norway 1-1, a goal by Craig Burley cancelling out one by Tore Andre Flo immediately after the start of the second half.

England lost their second game to Romania, the top seeds in their group. Both Romanian goals came from players based in England - Viorel Moldovan of Coventry City scored the first, which was pulled back in the 83rd minute by substitute Michael Owen. Just as both sides seemed to have settled for a draw, Dan Petrescu of Chelsea stuck his foot between Graeme Le Saux and goalkeeper David Seaman to grab all three points.

The eight games in the second round of the 1998 World Cup finals turned out as follows:

Italy *Vieri*	1	Norway	0
Brazil *Cesar Sampaio (2),* *Ronaldo (2, 1 penalty)*	4	**Chile** *Salas*	1
France *Blanc*	1	Paraguay	0
Nigeria *Babangida*	1	**Denmark** *Moller, Brian Laudrup, Sand,* *Helveg*	4
Germany *Klinsmann, Bierhoff*	2	Mexico *Hernandez*	1
Holland *Bergkamp, Davids*	2	**Yugoslavia** *Komljenovic*	1
Romania	0	Croatia *Suker (penalty)*	1
Argentina *Batistuta (penalty), Zanetti*	2	**England** *Shearer (penalty), Owen*	2

The match between France and Paraguay was the first in the history of the World Cup to be decided by the 'golden goal' method. Under this system, previously used in Euro '96, the team that wins is the one that scores first in extra time.

Germany left it very late against Mexico, after going behind in the 47th minute. Although they came through in the end, the Germans were widely thought to be struggling to paper the cracks in an old side - average age 31. Klinsmann gave everything, but the question remained: did he have enough left to get his side through another three high-pressure matches?

Holland almost lost to Yugoslavia, who were awarded a penalty but hit the crossbar with the kick. Edgar Davids' winner came in the last minute of normal time.

Croatia beat Romania thanks to Davor Suker, who remained calm when he had to retake his penalty kick because of encroachment in the area. He put the ball in the net both times.

The tie of the round was the match between Argentina and England. The South Americans went ahead through a penalty awarded against Seaman after six minutes, but England equalised four minutes later after Michael Owen was impeded in the Argentine area. Shearer scored from the resulting penalty.

England then took the lead with a goal from Owen, but Argentina made it 2-2 at half time when a cleverly worked free kick just outside the area was played through to Javier Zanetti.

At the start of the second half, David Beckham was sent off for retaliation after he had been fouled by Diego Simeone. The loss of a man greatly restricted England's capacity to attack, but they held out and seven minutes from time even had the ball in the Argentine net, but Sol Campbell's header was disallowed for a foul by Shearer on goalkeeper Carlos Roa.

After extra time produced no golden goal, the tie was decided on penalties. Argentina took the first and scored through Berti; Shearer made it 1-1, then Crespo's shot was saved by Seaman. Ince had the chance to make it 2-1 to England, but Roas saved his effort. Then Veron and Merson both scored to make it 2-2, and they were followed by Gallardo and Owen (3-3). Ayala made it 4-3 to Argentina and then David Batty's shot was saved by Roas. England were eliminated.

The quarter finals of the 1998 World Cup were between Holland and Argentina, Germany and Croatia, Italy and France and Brazil and Denmark.

Holland beat Argentina 2-1, with a goal by Patrick Kluivert after 12 minutes and a winner by Dennis Bergkamp from virtually the last kick of the game. In the meantime, the South Americans had equalised through Claudio Lopez.

Croatia beat a weary-looking Germany 3-0. Their goals were scored by Robert Jarni, Goran Vlaovic and Davor Suker. Germany had Christian Worns sent off.

Neither Italy nor France looked as if they would ever score, and they didn't. The tie was decided when Di Biagio missed in the penalty shoot-out.

Denmark took the lead against the favourites, Brazil, with a goal by Martin Jorgensen after two minutes. Brazil hit back through Bebeto and Rivaldo to take a half-time lead, but the Danes equalised after the break with a goal by Brian Laudrup. Brazil's winner was another goal for Rivaldo, whose speculative shot from outside the box evaded the dive of Peter Schmeichel.

In the first World Cup semi-final, Brazil beat Holland 4-2 on penalties after their match had ended 1-1 after extra time. Ronaldo had given Brazil the lead at the start of the second half, but Patrick Kluivert equalised three minutes from the end of normal time.

The 1998 World Cup

In the second semi-final, France came from a goal down to beat Croatia 2-1. Davor Suker gave the Croats the lead straight after half time but Lilian Thuram equalised immediately and then scored the winner in the 70th minute. France had Laurent Blanc sent off for hitting Slaven Bilic. Television replays suggested that although the Frenchman raised his hand and did make contact with his opponent, Bilic seemed to have made the most of the moment, as if wishing to draw the referee's attention to it.

The 1998 World Cup Final between the holders Brazil and the hosts France was held at the Stade de France, St Denis, Paris on July 12, 1998 in front of 80,000 spectators.

Brazil: Taffarel, Cafu, Aldair, Junior Baiano, Roberto Carlos, Leonardo (sub: Denilson), Cesar Sampaio (sub: Edmundo), Dunga, Rivaldo, Ronaldo, Bebeto
France: Barthez, Thuram, Desailly, Leboeuf, Lizarazu, Karembeu (sub: Boghossian), Deschamps, Petit, Zidane, Djorkaeff (sub: Vieira), Guivarc'h (sub: Dugarry)

Ronaldo had been unsure of his place until the last minute because of illness. He is thought to have suffered a fit on the morning of the match. His performance was subdued to say the least, and the French won 3-0 with two goals by Zinedine Zidane and one in the last minute by Emmanuel Petit. Marcel Desailly was sent off for two bookable offences.

Leading scorer in the 1998 World Cup finals was Davor Suker, with six goals for Croatia, who finished in third place.

Suker's closest challengers for the Golden Boot were Gabriel Batistuta of Argentina and Christian Vieri of Italy, who both finished the tournament with five goals. Ronaldo of Brazil, Marcelo Salas of Chile and Luis Hernandez of Mexico all scored four.